TRUST ISSUES

Manage the Anxiety, Insecurity, and Jealousy in Your Relationship with 10 Simple Steps

4th EDITION

BY

JESSICA RILEY

The trademarks that are used are without any consent, and the publication of the trademark is without permission or backing by the trademark owner.

All trademarks as well as brands within this book are for clarifying purposes only and are the owned by the owners themselves, not affiliated with this document.

Contents

Introduction

There is nothing that will end a relationship faster than jealousy. Whether it is the kind of jealousy where someone is upset their significant other is conversing with someone they perceive to be prettier, smarter, or overall better in some way or they are jealous because they feel they've lost control of the situation, it all leads to the same thing. Jealousy is the infamous green-eyed monster that will end a relationship quicker than or just as quick as one partner cheating on the other.

Where there is jealousy, there is also anxiety and insecurity, the three of these things tend to go hand in hand. Anxiety is the emotion a jealous person is actually experiencing, while insecurity is the nagging at the back of their mind that insists they must see phone message, emails and have an explanation for every second that their partner was late getting home. Jealousy is exhausting for both sides of the team, and it's also unfair to both partners.

Luckily, there is a way to recognize when jealousy is the problem at hand. And, if jealousy is to blame, there are simple steps that you can take to suppress those feelings and get back into the only game you should be in, the game of love.

In this book, you will find a comprehensive guide on how to understand what you are feeling, along with how you can deal with it in an adult manner.

The ten steps to eradicating trust issues are:

- Understanding the difference between feeling jealous and acting jealous.

- Assessing your situation and yourself.

- Believing in your partner.

- Comparing yourself to others.

- Being prepared to lose your partner.

- Ending the jealousy games.

- Halting that overactive imagination.

- Letting go.

- Imagining a positive, self-confident you.

- Reminding yourself of your positive traits.

In this book there are also some special chapters that have been included to help you understand how to handle trust issues in specific scenarios. You will learn what you should do when you are in a long distance relationship, how to handle trust with someone who has mental disabilities and even how to handle financial infidelity.

After completing this book, you might like to comeback and read it again. While that might not be a bad idea I also have a little bit of advice, something that I like to encourage in my students, write notes on what you've already read, so you can soak it in better.

Chapter One:
Understanding the Difference between Feeling Jealous and Acting Jealous

When a relationship first starts out, there is a period of time where you learn to love each other. You begin by evaluating your positive and negative attributes and deciding that you will still be with the person, regardless of the attributes. During this time, you begin to enjoy their constant attention and presence, but you also start to experience feelings of apprehension when they are not with you. You fall in love, and with that other feelings begin to emerge.

One of those feelings you will experience is jealousy. Jealousy is a natural reaction to anything that you view as a threat, but it is most pronounced in relationships. If you feel that someone or something is going to take your partner away from you, then anxiety and jealousy begin to take root. However, it is how you act on these feelings that will determine whether you are extremely insecure or if you fully trust your partner.

Once you experience jealousy, you then have the option of acting upon your feelings. Feeling jealousy is internal, whereby you assess the situation, experience the feeling, but do nothing to move on it. Acting jealous is external. It happens after you feel jealousy, and then you make the decision to take a course of action, so that you can feel better about the situation or control the situation.

To understand the difference between feeling jealous and acting jealous, we will use an example.

You are sitting at a restaurant or a bar with your significant other, and you happen to see their eyes stray to someone whom you perceive to be more attractive than you. Even if you do not feel threatened by that other person, you might be a little annoyed by your partner's distinct loss of attention being trained on you. This is the moment where the green-eyed monster might make its appearance, but in truth, you are just feeling jealousy, you have yet to act on those feelings. Your mind runs through a variety of scenarios about what might happen if the perceived threat shows an interest in your partner.

When you act on those feelings, you lose faith in your partner's ability to control themselves, you expect that they will hurt your feelings and give in to any temptation. If you do not act upon that jealousy and that insecurity, and recognize it for what it is, then youare not *being* jealous or insecure; this is an indication that there is a strong foundation of trust in your relationship. However, if you do choose to take action on your feelings of jealousy, then you are acting jealous and revealing weakness and insecurity in your relationship.

There are different ways that you can act on your jealousy. These include confronting your partner on their wandering eye and possible inappropriate thoughts (which reveals your insecurities), giving your partner the silent treatment (often without explaining why), or even throwing a tantrum or threatening the person you believe is a threat to your relationship.Insecurity opens the door to a whole host of problems, plus insecurity manifests and expresses itself in a very negative way.

Now that you have an understanding between acting jealous and feeling jealous, it is time to look at jealousy in general and how it affects your relationship. One of the first things that you need to understand is that jealous affects everybody at some point in their lives; it is how you react to the jealousy that can cause future problems. Where jealousy becomes a major problem is where it begins to take over your entire life, basically when all you can think about is what others have that you don't.

Can you really overcome jealousy?

Even knowing what jealousy is many people are often left with the question, as to whether they can overcome it or not. If this is you, don't worry, there is a way to overcome jealousy so that you can start to rebuild the trust in your relationship.

One of the first steps to overcoming the problem of jealousy is to admit that you have a problem. Admitting you have a problem simply means your jealous feelings are taking total control over your life. They are so bad that they are actually preventing you from being happy with your current life choices, including your current relationship. However, the biggest problem with jealousy is how it can prevent you and your partner from reaching your goals.

One of the first things you need to do is determine if these jealous feelings are taking over your life or if they are just your normal run of the meal issues that everybody else is dealing with. So, how can you tell the difference? Easy look for any of these signs:

- All of your time is spent wishing you had everything that others had

- You are constantly comparing yourself to others and coming up short.

- Can't spend too much time with certain people because you always feel badly about yourself because you are not good enough.

- Have a hard time accepting the fact that your partner has friends besides you.

- Never enjoy a night out with your partner because you feel like everybody around you is better than you.

Where is it coming from?

Once you know that you have a problem, you need to figure out where the problem is coming from. This is going to require you to look deep within yourself, which can be quite painful. You need to figure out what it is that is making you jealous, what happened to you before to cause these kinds of feelings. Knowing where the feelings are coming from is the only hope you have in understand what needs to be fixed in your relationship, as well as how to go about fixing it.

With how many different reasons people have to be jealous of others, it can be kind of difficult getting started. To help you narrow down the most likely causes of where the feelings are coming from here are some things you can look at:

- Material things – If you are jealous of all of the material things that people have that can still have adverse effects on your relationship. The reason behind that is you are never going to feel like you have enough and those negative thoughts are going to take a toll. You need to work on how you view yourself to solve this kind of a problem.

- How others look – If you are concerned that you don't look as good as other people that is going to slowly eat away at your relationship. It is going to affect every aspect of it because you will never be happy when going out on dates and you will always be second guessing things. To help solve this issue you can work on improving your own looks by dieting and exercising. Or better yet you can focus on your best features and work on reminding yourself you are worth loving.

- Relationships – This is probably the most common problem when it comes to jealousy. If you find yourself worried about other relationships that your partner might have, there is a serious problem. If you are jealous of others' relationships, to the point you wish yours was like theirs, it is time to do some serious evaluating of your own relationship to determine if it is something that is really worth saving.

Jealousy is often suggested to be a very negative emotion, though in effect, it is simply worry masked in angry agitation. The interesting thing about jealousy is that it is only the person who is feeling it who can relate to it. When expressed to the person it is directed to, they are often left confused, and in some cases even afraid, of what is happening with their partner.

This is particularly true if jealousy leads an insecure person to start questioning their partner. Some of the more common questions asked by an insecure partner include, but are not limited to:

- Am I still attractive?

- Do you still love me?

- Will you ever leave me?

Jealousy within a relationship can lead a generally rational person into exhibiting some extremely irrational or even crazy behavior, which all too often creates problems within the relationship.

Problems in a relationship normally start when you lose all trust for your partner, when you do not believe in anything that they may have to tell you. You may begin to follow your partner around after they call you to let you know they are going to be late home from work or when they do something that seems to be out of their normal routine. Things only get worse, as you find that you have to know who they were just on the phone with because you are afraid it might be another woman or man. You start imaging the worst, such as they might be planning to leave you.

These are all indications that you are feeling vulnerable and insecure as a result of being jealous and unable to communicate your feelings. Your partner is unable to have any privacy when it comes to what they're doing. Believe me it's not that they don't want to tell you; it's that you demand to know in a manner that makes them feel as if you don't trust them.

At this point, your partner will start to shut down, and communication may come to a standstill. This kind of situation spells the beginning of hardship in your relationship, especially if your partner is perfectly innocent of anything you may have accused them of. They may feel deeply hurt that you would harbor such ill thoughts of them; they may even decide that no matter how good they are to you, you will continue to distrust them.

Let's face it, the jealousy, insecurity, and anxiety all come down to one thing: trust. Is there trust between both people in the relationship?

If you arealways worrying about your partner straying, you have trust issues. More than anything, these need to be addressed; otherwise the future of the relationship is shaky. Fortunately, there's good news. You've picked up this book because you realize that you have these types of issues, or you know that your partner is experiencing this.

So how can you tell the difference between reasonable concern and extreme jealousy or mistrust? If you've started the behavior of tracking down your partner's every move because you are afraid they will cheat on you or verifying every statement they tell you because you believe that they are dishonest; then you are acting jealous, insecure, and anxious.In a healthy and balanced relationship, you would be able to ask your partner about their whereabouts, and trust that the response you receive is the complete truth. In a healthy relationship, you will also have a reasonable amount of self-esteem, which would mean that you value yourself enough to believe that you are exactly what your partner needs, so they have no reason to stray.

While doing some detective work might get you some quick answers as to whether or not your partner has strayed, it will not give you the emotional satisfaction that you need. This is because if you start fishing around for something negative in your relationship, you are sure to stumble across some dirt because no one is perfect. If in fact you do not stumble across any negative information, you may misinterpret the existing information, so that it can fit into the scenario you were expecting in your mind. The truth is, you are asking yourself a question that you may not even want to acknowledge.

That question is..."If I ask my partner to love me and make me feel secure in our relationship, will they do that, or will they leave me?"

There are many questions that couples need to ask each other when they choose to remain committed to each other. When dealing with jealousy, if you are unable to ask your partner this question, then you will develop even more insecurities that will simply develop into a more serious problem. You need to realize that your partner is not responsible for making you feel a certain way. You must be right with yourself first, you need to address the reasons you feel insecure and anxious, so that you can overcome the problems jealousy has caused in your relationship. Doing so will allow you to establish an active path leading towards total trust.

Here is a list of things that you can look for to determine if you or your partner are suffering from insecurity:

- You or they want to see emails, access social networks, go through the correspondence either party has with other people, or insist that you should have access to each other's passwords.

- You are unable to have a phone conversation without them in the room, or you have to be there for all phone conversations.

- When your partner calls home to let you knowthey are going to be late, or vice versa, then there's a fight because you do not trust your partner or vice versa.

- You feel anxious when your partner goes out with friends and wonder whether they will meet someone who may lead them astray.

- You feel insecure when your partner talks with other people, especially if they are of the opposite sex.

While it is healthy and expected that you will experience some jealous thoughts, you should be able to speak openly with your partner about them. Speaking openly about them is what allows you to overcome them completely. To establish trust in your relationship, communication is key. By talking about your feelings, especially your jealous feelings, you empower both yourself and your partner. Acting on your jealousy can have disastrous results; wrong accusations can damage the very foundation of your relationship.

Rather than acting on your jealousy by embarking on detective work, or projecting your insecurity through accusations, take the time to discuss your feelings of jealousy with your partner before they begin to spiral completely out of your control.

Ways to Handle Your Jealousy

Now we have already discussed how jealousy can affect your relationship, but what we haven't really talked about is how you can go about handling your jealousy. While in the beginning stages of your relationship, the over possessive behavior might be welcome, but the further your relationship progresses, the more unwelcome the behavior becomes. Many partners feel in the beginning that the jealousy is nice; they think that it shows how much their partner cares about them. However, as time goes on and the jealousy continues, it usually transpires into something neither party wants to deal with.

The more jealous you become, the more your partner is going to pull away. After the newness of the relationship wears off, jealousy doesn't seem like caring any longer. Basically, the more possessive you get the more trapped your partner is going to feel. Now don't get us wrong, jealousy on occasion can add something to a relationship, but what you need to do is know when and how to handle your jealousy, so that it doesn't destroy your relationship.

Trusting your partner

Now this one might seem kind of obvious, but it is the biggest step when trying to deal with jealousy. As a highly jealous person, chances are you are going to be suspicious of everything that your partner says. However, all that is doing is creating a bad situation; you are simply setting your relationship up to fail. Nobody wants to have what they say questioned, so you need to start taking your partner's word for things. Sure, it's going to be hard to do that, it's not a change that is going to happen overnight, but you must do it. In the beginning, you might find it helpful if you simply just start acting like you believe them, regardless of if you do or not. In time, you will find yourself actually believing them. If you have been checking up on them, quit doing it. If they tell you something, believe them.

Quit Comparing Yourself

One of the biggest reasons people are jealous is because of their own low self-esteem. These kinds of people constantly feel like they are never good enough for anybody or anything. What you need to remember is everybody is different. Sure, there are going to be people out there who have more money than you or who are even funnier than you are, but don't worry about it. Your partner picked you for a reason. You need to quit focusing on the reasons why they won't like you and instead focus on the fact that they simply love you for you.

Never Play Games

This is probably the most destructive thing you can ever do in a relationship. Sadly, it is something that goes on just about every day. Some people are simply not content with just being jealous, so they do everything in their power to make their partner feel jealous. Don't take your issues out on your partner. The last thing they want to see is you acting like a fool by flirting with others in front of them.

Honestly, it usually ends up backfiring on you anyway. Chances are your partner won't get jealous, they will just get mad. At the same time, this doesn't mean to pretend that good looking people don't exist, as we all know they do. What you need to do is learn how to not use them to harm your relationship. Plus, if things do go sour, your partner cannot use these kinds of things against you, when the relationship ends.

Quit Mixing up Your Imagination with Reality

Having an overactive imagination can be fun, just think about all the things you can picture inside your head with one. The problem though, is when you are in a relationship and your overactive imagination, takes the place of reality. It's so easy to get caught up in things we imagine in our heads, to the point that we eventually start to think these things are real, which can impact our relationships. You need to stop believing everything your mind dreams up, imagination is never the same thing as reality. The sooner you get this figured out, the sooner you can start effectively dealing with your jealousy.

Give Your Partner Some Freedom

This can be said in many different terms, but it all boils down to giving your partner the freedom that they deserve. Jealousy, all too often, consumes the entire relationship, you worry so much about what the other party is doing that you want to spend every waking moment with them to make sure they are not doing something wrong. Sure, it's nice to spend time with your partner, but every waking moment is taking things a bit too far. Give them the freedom they deserve, don't fight them going out with friends, and don't let it bother you when they talk to other people when they are out with you.

Use Your Imagination for Good Not Bad

Now this might seem a little strange, but your overactive imagination can actually help you get a handle on your jealousy. Most of us with jealousy issues let our imaginations run wild. We imagine our partner doing something to hurt us, no matter how innocent the situation can be. To help get a handle on your jealousy, you need to take your thoughts to another level. Imagine your relationship coming to an end, then think about how your life would be if you were no longer in that relationship. Visualize just how fine your life will be, just in case the worst actually happens.

You can also use your overactive imagination in another manner. Allow yourself to imagine all of the scenarios possible involving your partner and what you think they are doing. Now put yourself into the scene, but picture yourself not reacting to what they are doing. Visualize yourself being calm while they are flirting with somebody else. Picture these scenarios and your reaction several times a day. The more you practice the sooner you will be able to control your jealousy.

Your Jealous Partner

So far, this chapter has addressed what it means to handle your jealousy for your partner, but what happens if you are the person on the receiving end of a jealous partner? Trust in a relationship goes two ways, as just as you might be dealing with issues around jealousy, your partner may have also developed similar problems. It must be said that it is much easier to deal with your won jealousy to build the trust in your relationship than it is to deal with the jealousy of another person. Here is what you can expect from your partner who is dealing with feeling jealous.

Suspicion

You will constantly be under the microscope. Your partner will find it challenging to believe in anything that you have to say, and the actions that you take to offer them reassurance. There will be nothing that you can do right. You should be prepared for your communication devices and tools to be under consistent scrutiny, and if for any reason you do something that is out of the ordinary, you should be ready for the backlash.

Be prepared for your relationships with others to be analyzed and diced up in an attempt to find you at some wrong doing. Even something innocent between you and a family member could be misconstrued. You feel at a complete loss to resolve the problem.

There are some points that you should remember when dealing with jealousy, especially when your partner is jealous. The first is that you cannot change the person or solve their jealousy issue for them. It is their issue, and you may not be fully aware where it finds its roots. There are some things that you can do to help the situation, and also help you to keep your sanity as you consistently build the trust in your union. These things include: -

- Being fully aware of any possible way that you may be contributing to the issue. There may be some things that you are doing that are being misconstrued by your partner, even if this is not your intention. Begin by honestly evaluating your behavior in the situation that you are in, and ask yourself some compelling questions. The first of these questions should be: -

  Is there anything that I have done to trigger my partner's jealousy? Has your partner witnessed you flirting with other people?

  Even when you are doing something that is seemingly innocent to you, you need to be aware of what you partner may consider to be not innocent. You may be the trigger for the jealousy, so you can work on correcting your behavior before you confront your partner. You may find that simply acknowledging your behavior and changing it could be all the difference.

- Approach your partner with love and kindness to reestablish the trust that you had originally. Remember that you are likely dealing with a partner who has insecurity, and wants to feel as though their insecurity is justified and you are responsible for the issues that they are facing. Therefore, if they can lead you into an argument that veers off topic, then you will end up more frustrated and they end up feeling justified. Either way, the relationship does not benefit.

  It may feel uncomfortable taking the approach of love, especially if your privacy has been violated. So what you need to do is set some boundaries that help to stop the jealous behavior of your partner. As you accepted responsibility before, you need to get your partner to accept responsibility for their inappropriate behavior through a calm discussion. At this point you must be firm about what you believe to be acceptable and what is not. Speak from your own perspective, and do not make assumptions about what your partner really wants. Ensure that you both fit within certain boundaries, so that whatever your partner chooses to do to you, you can do to them as well.

- Do not spare your feelings, let your partner know how their jealousy is affecting your relationship, and also that if they are unable to find a way to handle it, you may not stick around for the accusations to come. You need to do this calmly and without argument, no matter what reaction or outburst that your partner displays.

At the same time, offer your partner your support in helping them to identify ways that they can overcome the jealousy that seems to be eating the, up. You need to let your partner know that they need to face their jealousy, and let it go.

Living with a jealous partner can be difficult and puts an incredible strain on the relationship. It affects overall happiness for both parties, especially when the jealousy is unwarranted.

Getting a handle on your jealousy isn't as easy as it might sound. While some of the methods might seem pretty straight forward, there is a lot of work that goes into each step. And, because of that we will discuss each of these methods in more detail throughout this book.

Chapter Two:
Assessing the Situation

Part 1: Assessing Your Relationship

There is a reason that you are in your current relationship, and most likely this reason revolves around love, more than it does jealousy. Before you committed to your relationship, you were able to look past any negativity and see only the positive sides of your partner. Your relationship was based on positivity, good loving memories and heartwarming experiences. Over time though, feelings of jealousy may have started to creep in, and may have reached the point where you do not know how to handle or control these feelings.

You may be feeling jealous because you are in a relationship where jealousy, insecurity, and anxiety flourish. Jealousy begins to creep in when you feel as though you have been let down in some way, something occurred which did not meet your expectations.

Think about how you and your partner behave toward one another, and then try to figure out why you are feeling this way toward your partner, or why your partner is feeling this way towards you. Are there things that you did with your partner at the beginning of the relationship which you no longer do? Or perhaps your communication has taken a nose dive and you find it difficult to express yourself? Have you learned something about your partners past that may explain their behavior in the present?

No matter what the question is you need to be honest in your evaluation, lying to yourself is only going to make things worse. Keep in mind that relationships naturally go through highs and lows. It is often during the lows that insecurities are exposed and jealousy takes root.

If you're the jealous partner, perhaps you feel this way because someone hurt you in the past. You may also love your partner so much that even just the thought of losing them makes you panic. Good or bad, we are shaped by our experiences. We naturally create defense mechanisms to protect us when we are hurt. The most common of these defense mechanisms is jealousy, which is what you express when you are trying to control a situation. When everything is going well in your relationship, you are unlikely to experience jealousy, but all it takes is one little incident and memories from betrayal in your past come rushing back. It is at this point that you imagine all the different ways your partner can betray you and jealousy begins to take root.

There are many different ways in which you can be hurt in a relationship, being lied to is just one of those ways. Catching your partner in a lie can be pretty devastating to a relationship, especially if you trusted your partner and discovered that they willingly took part in something to deceive you or even cheat you in some way. If you have experienced this behavior, it may be hard, but try to put it in the past and remember that this is a different person. Even if they have different behavior, you may still harbor feelings of betrayal and question why anyone would even stray in the first place. Everyone behaves differently in a relationship, judging your partner on your previous partner's behaviors is not fair.

If you area person who has a jealous partner, try to talk to them about why they are acting the way they are. It is entirely normal to react to their jealous behavior, but you need to try your best not to, reacting to the behavior is going to do nothing but cause more problems. A perfect example is when

26

you react to their behavior by doing something that will make them jealous, acting this way is beneath you and is not the way to solve the jealousy problem at hand.

You need to approach your partner from an empathetic viewpoint because jealousy is just misguidedworry that is clouded with anger. You should look at them with some compassion, and attempt to understand what may be the actual cause of their jealous feelings. They may have been cheated on in the past, which would in all honesty affect their viewpoint on future relationships. Bring this to the forefront; be honest about how you feel in order for them to get a good idea of what their behavior is doing to your relationship.

You should also evaluate your own behavior as you may have inadvertently acted in a way that sparked their jealousy. Perhaps without realizing it, you have been emotionally or even physically unfaithful to your partner, which has sparked their insecurity and led to mistrust and jealousy. They may believe that you have been unfaithful to them, even though in your opinion this is not the case. Try to be understanding because a breakup due to cheating can be very detrimental to a person's self-esteem.

When it comes to talking about love, honesty is the best way to go. Open communication will help solve issues before they even become issues.

Part 2: Assessing Yourself

If you are currently in a relationship that was built on honesty, security, and trust, you need to ask yourself why you are feeling jealous and insecure when you do not have a reason to. Explore your life experiences and think back about your childhood. It may seem silly, but people who developed secure relationships with their primary caregivers often have stable relationships during their adult lives. You may have had an adverse incident at some point in your life and not even realized it. Many times adverse incidents remain firmly in your subconscious. People who experience adverse incidents tend to have self-esteem issues later on in life.

Jealousy is often based on more than just the situation at hand. It is similar to an iceberg, you see the tip of it above the water, but this does not tell you how deep or wide the iceberg is underneath. There is a reason that you would feel threatened enough that it affects your relationship. Ask yourself some of the following questions to better understand your relationship style (secure or insecure):

- Do you feel empty or lack self-worth?

- How was your relationship with your parents or guardians?

- Did warmth and love surround your early childhood or was it stressful?

- Were you raised in an atmosphere that was oppressive?

- Were your parents or guardians unreliable when you were a child?

- Do you hold your partner responsible for how you are feeling?

- Have you tried to control your partner's behavior so that you can feel less anxious?

Your answers to these questions will help you better understand your psyche, so make sure you are answering honestly. And, don't worry nobody but you, will know the answers to these important questions, unless you feel the need to share.

The deeper you explore your answers, the more likely you are to identify the key incidents that shaped you into the person you are today, which your answers will also explain how these events affect your behavior today. Perhaps as a child your parents divorced and did not explain things to you very well. You may have taken that on as your fault, or wondered why they met other people. You then carry this baggage into your current relationship, and in a way, make your partner the bad guy, always waiting for the day that they will walk out and divorce you. This could lead to jealous and anxious behavior that could confuse your partner and ultimately cause your relationship to suffer.

Answering these questions can help you identify incidences, but can also help you realistically view your behavior, so you can see how it is affecting your current relationship, for better or worse. In order to establish trust, you need to have a clear idea of the situation that you are facing, starting with knowing who you are in the relationship. You will also need to understand what you had in the very beginning of the relationship, what you had that allowed trust to begin building.

Something that you want to bear in mind is that jealousy may have existed in your relationship for so long, that you are not even sure whether you are the jealous one or if it your partner who is exhibiting those traits. If this is the case, you can ask yourself some questions that will make you think about the depth of the problem, along with where it lies. These questions could include:

1. Do you get furious and panic when you do not hear from your partner for a few hours?

2. Are you constantly texting and calling your partner to know their whereabouts?

3. Are you constantly questioning your partner about whether they find others attractive?

4. Do you come up with elaborate schemes on how you can catch your partner betraying you?

5. Feel terrible if your partner admires a famous person?

If you answered yes to any of these questions, then sadly the problem lies with you in that you are the one exhibiting the behaviors. If you are the one with the jealousy issues, you need to make some drastic changes. To start you will want to evaluate why you feel the way you do in specific situations, what is causing you to be jealous. Are you unhappy with your looks? Do you feel bad about your financial situation? No matter the reason you need to work on changing the way you feel about yourself, so you can address your jealousy issues and move forward with a healthy relationship.

Identifying Toxic Behaviors

When dealing with trust issues within your relationship, jealousy is probably the biggest problem. After all, if you are jealous of the attention your partner is giving others, what you are self-consciously saying is you don't trust that person to do right by you. Even if you make the claim that it's the other people you don't trust, you are basically saying you don't trust your partner, remember it takes more than one person to create any kind of situation.

While jealousy might be a big issue, it is not the only reason for trust issues in a relationship. Insecurities are another big problem in relationships, but an even bigger problem is all of the other toxic behaviors that are not often talked about. No matter what kind of toxic behavior you are dealing with, and regardless of whether it is you or your partner exhibiting these behaviors, all they succeed in doing is pushing you away from one another. And, we all know how devastating that behavior can be, as we have seen our share of relationships end from this exact behavior.

Now, if you are honest with yourself you will freely admit that you have engaged in some kind of toxic manner before, even if it was against your better judgment. Even the most positive people suffer from mood swings on occasion. It's those of us who view the world in a more negative light that cause the most damage to ourselves and those we love with our toxic behaviors.

Now, no matter how often you experience these crazy mood swings it is important to immediately identify these toxic behaviors. The sooner you identify these toxic behaviors, the better, as your chances of resolving the trust issues in your relationship will drastically improve when you get rid of the behaviors that are responsible for the problems. Not only that, but your relationship's long-term happiness rests on your ability to change your negative behavior into positive behavior.

Don't know what to look for, let us help. Here is a brief look at 12 toxic behaviors you need to erase from your life today.

Envy

Envy is quite similar to jealousy, many people even use the terms interchangeably. What you need to learn to recognize is when you are envious of somebody or something. Being envious causes you to lose sight of what is important in your life and your relationship, as you are too worried about what those around you have. Remind yourself to be thankful for what you have in your life. Remember your life and your relationship is not a competition, all you can do is be the best person and partner you can be. Never compare yourself or your relationship to others, simply compare it to what it was yesterday.

Playing the Victim

One thing that drives people insane is when people constantly play the victim. One of the worst things about this kind of toxic behavior is that it is a hard one to get out of. People often find themselves stuck in it because they simply have no desire to move forward in their lives. These people are perfectly content with constantly complaining about their lives or their relationships. It's kind of like the poor me cycle, only worse because you lack the drive to help yourself. Truth is, we all have it in ourselves to rise above our situation and make a positive change. The sooner you do, the sooner you can move on from this debilitating behavior.

Taking Things Personally

Now sure everybody is going to get offended at one time or another, but it grows tiring when you are constantly offended by everything that is said or done around them. You need to step back and remind yourself that the world does not revolve around you. People's thoughts and actions are not a direct reflection on you. In all honesty, how people talk and act around you is based on their life experiences, not yours. What you need to do is not worry too much about other's opinions of you, whether they are good or bad, and focus instead on doing your own thing.

Constant Negative Thinking

Nobody likes the poor pity me person, but even more loathed than that person is the person that is always being negative. Majority of people simply don't want to be around negative people because it starts to take a toll on them. People like this fail to see anything positive happening, for them it's all about the negative. And, if you think about it that is a pretty messed up way to view the world, let alone your relationship. Adopting a positive attitude, which is discussed later on in this book, is the best way to rid yourself of this toxic behavior.

No Emotional Self-Control

Emotional self-control means being able to maintain total control over all of your emotions. People with emotional self-control do not suffer from extreme outbursts of emotions, including, but not limited to, anger and sadness. It's easy to spot the people who have no emotional self-control, as they are often yelling or screaming in anger at somebody for something that is beyond that person's control. A perfect example of this is somebody yelling at a cashier for a long line at the grocery store. If this sounds like you, it is best to seek some kind of help to sort out your emotional issues.

Judging Others

Although making judgments is part of human nature that doesn't mean it is a good thing to do. Majority of us judge others by what we are shown, such as a person who dresses a specific way, we automatically assume something about them based on how they are dressed. What your mom or even grandma used to tell you about not judging a book by its cover is very wise advice. People only show others what they want them to see. You never really know what they are going through, and judging them superficially because of something they did or said, should be avoided at all costs. If you catch yourself judging your partner, stop immediately and redirect your thinking. Take the time to go up to them, talk to them about what is going on rather than assume.

Not Letting Go

No matter if it is pain or loss you are holding onto, it is far more destructive for your relationship than you realize. Yes, it's hard to let go of some things and move on, we have all been there, but for the sake of your relationship, it is something that you have to do, especially if you want to be able to move forward. You need to work on setting yourself free from the emotional entanglements of the past, including, but not limited to, previous relationships. Breaking free from the past will allow you to move forward in a positive way with your current relationship. Changing the way you think isn't going to be easy, but it will be worth it.

Striving For Perfection

While it's normal for you to strive for perfection in certain aspects of your life, that doesn't mean it is right. No matter if, you are after the perfect house, the perfect job, or even the perfect relationship, what you need to remember is that perfection doesn't really exist. People are constantly changing and adapting to events that happen in their lives, so relationships have to constantly evolve and adapt. If you want the relationship to work, you have to realize that it is an imperfect relationship, but with time and effort, it can be the best relationship for you. You have to rid yourself of thinking that the "perfect" person is out there for you because who they are today, might not be who they are tomorrow.

Always Needing Validation

The last thing your partner wants to do is constantly reassure you that they love you and care about you. Constantly having to validate their feelings for you proves to be exhausting. And, if you are caught in having to constantly prove yourself to others to feel worthy of yourself, you end up bringing down those around you. You are silently sending the message that you are superior to them, even if that isn't what you are trying to say at all. Remember, there is more to life than proving yourself to everybody around you. If you catch yourself seeking the validation of others, change the direction of your thoughts, redirect the attention away from you, and instead focus it on the bigger picture.

Being Mean

Being mean to others is one of the worst toxic behaviors around. How this usually comes about is that you have no compassion for those around you. Instead, you simply lash out at whoever is around because you can. Nobody wants to be with somebody who is going to tear them down just to make themselves feel or look better. Being mean and spiteful is not the way to have a healthy and loving relationship. Luckily, if you are exhibiting this toxic behavior in your relationship as a way to cover the hurt from the past, there is still hope. You can change your behavior by stopping yourself the minute you hear yourself tearing somebody down. Redirect your thoughts and find some compassion in your heart for whomever it is you are tearing down.

Hiding Your True Self

If you never let your partner see the real you, there is no way you are ever going to form a connection with them. This might seem kind of pointless, but it becomes a huge problem if your partner grows attached to the "fake" you. Pretending to be someone you are not is the same as lying to your partner, which is not going to help with the trust issues in the relationship. Instead embrace who you are and let your partner see the real you.

Cheating

Cheating does not just apply to having affairs in relationships, although that is a very big one. As a toxic behavior, cheating is cutting corners or taking shortcuts whenever you can, simply because you can. What you need to remember about any kind of cheating is that it is something that you choose to do; you cannot later on try to say it was a mistake, as you made the conscience decision to do it. The problem with cheating is it destroys your partners trust in you. Always be the better person, doing the right thing will only build up the trust in your relationship.

Just remember you are not alone when it comes to exhibiting toxic behaviors. Everybody exhibits some kind of toxic behavior during their life. What is important is that you learn to recognize these damaging behaviors and stop them before they can take too strong of a hold.

Chapter Three:
Believing Your Partner

There is a saying that goes, "Shame on you if you fool me once, shame on me if you fool me twice." This ties in with what it takes to build and maintain trust in a relationship. When someone does something that you do not like, or that does not meet your expectations, then you are likely to forgive them. Should they repeat the action or something similar a second time, then trust starts to go out the window. From then on, the person is often reminded of their inability to keep their word, they are always judged based on what happened previously. When this happens, relationships change, and the accused or guilty party may find themselves unwilling to invest in the relationship, as the results are not always positive.

When you stop giving your partner a chance to redeem themselves, then you have undoubtedly also stopped believing in your partner. It is at this juncture that trust is not there. Whatever they may tell you, a small voice in your head will start to speak up about how you might not be able to trust what your partner is saying. Then before you know what has happened, there is frustration, discord, and pain in your relationship. This is the point where you begin to get suspicious, and your thoughts can then negatively affect your actions.

Sometimes you may feel you know something about a person or a situation, even when you have no evidence to back up your thoughts. You believe in putting two and two together, you have a cause and effect reference section in your mind where you try to understand a situation by adding up all of the variables. This is what you will be doing all the time if you do not believe in your partner. Everything that they say to you will appear to be a lie. If they do not behave the way you expect, you will think that they are deliberately being dishonest. You will find yourself constantly checking for anything out of the ordinary.

Perhaps you are cringing right now because this is your worst fear, but let's look at why that makes you afraid. Jealousy stems from a lack of trust and fear; it is rooted in worry and expressed through agitated anger. It causes insecurity and anxiety in a relationship, and will ultimately eradicate all chances of you having a healthy partnership with your significant other.

When you are jealous, insecure, and anxious, you are permanently on the lookout for alleged lies or inconsistencies from your partner. You wait for them to slip up, and relish catching them; proving that your worries were founded. Your feelings at this juncture are rooted in fear, and though you try to find evidence to back up your assumptions, you do so with your heart constantly racing due to anticipation. You want to know "the truth", yet you are afraid to do so. So why are you afraid?

People who are jealous in a relationship fear more than just losing their partner. They fear losing their self-respect and the respect of others if they have been in a relationship where cheating was the primary cause of the breakup. They are afraid of being mocked and laughed at by their peers. They may also be afraid of looking naïve and foolish. Most of all, they may fear that they will eventually end up completely alone. While this can be understood in relationships where cheating has happened before, unfounded jealousy is detrimental to your current relationship, and it will continue to plague you unless you take control of it now.

Taking Control of your Emotions in your Relationship

The first step to taking control of your jealousy is to understand and acknowledge that you are distrustful of your partner. This will stop you from blaming them for your feelings and expecting them to do something to resolve the situation. Once you can acknowledge your feelings, you empower yourself to take action and resolve them.

From the moment that you understand that you are making a conscious decision to be jealous, you can release that anxiety and fear and decide to trust your partner. You may begin by looking at your partner with a fresh set of eyes; viewing all their actions from a definite point of view, rather than from a doubtful and negative point of view. This is not as easy as it may sound, but it can be done.

You could also opt to wipe the slate clean and start afresh. This means that you choose to leave the past in the past, and look at your partner from all the deeds that they do starting now. Although difficult, living in the moment can be very liberating. If you have no suspicion or background worries, then you are better able to trust and believe your partner when they tell you something or give you any other information. You will not prejudge their behavior, and you will not make yourself miserable remembering painful memories.

Next time your partner calls to let you know they will be working late, let them know that it is okay and hang up the phone. Whereby in the past your conversation may have included numerous questions such as where they are, who they are with, what they are doing, why they are doing this to you, you can choose to ask a different set of questions. You may ask questions like whether they are ok, have they had something to eat or would they like a warm bath when they get home. These issues are unlikely to put your partner on the defensive, in fact, they could have them rushing to finish whatever is keeping them so they can come home to a loving atmosphere.

Following the phone call, instead of sitting down and allowing your imagination to go wild thinking of them with another person, visualize them doing what they claim to be doing. So, if your partner said that they are in the office, picture them sitting at their computer and working hard. This way, when they come home, they are likely to find a more relaxed person, who is looking to help them get a load of stress off their shoulders, rather than someone who has worked themselves up into a paranoid frenzy, hitting them with a barrage of questions before they have even gotten through the front door.

Resist the urge to call them a second time half an hour later to see where they are, and don't check their phone when they get home to see what they may have been up to. Instead, start to train your mind to believe what they have told you. If this has not been the way your relationship has previously functioned, it will be difficult. However, you must realize that this is not an immediate process with instant results. It will require daily effort and you will probably start by taking small steps until you have built up enough of your own self confidence to trust your partner 100%.

The next time your partner asks for your trust, give it to them. Although this might be difficult and you may doubt that they deserve it, giving them the trust they need is the best way to get trustworthy behavior back from them. The probable effect of this behavior is that your partner will be more likely to open up to you, and give you information on what they have been up to, even before you have had a chance to ask. This would be because they no longer feel trapped, they have been empowered to make their own decisions, and they are experiencing a new way of communication and behavior within the relationship.

Remember that if they break your trust and they lie to you, then they're not making a fool out of you. They're making a fool out of themselves. In this case, they are the ones doing damage to the relationship, and you would be justified in making the decision to leave. You are not responsible for their behavior; you are only responsible for your own, including how you react to any indiscretion on their part.

Trust is the cornerstone of a relationship. If you have a trustworthy partner, and are the one experiencing problems with insecurities, accusing your partner of cheating or lying is extremely insulting. The constant barrage of questions from you is just as detrimental to a relationship as an affair would be. If your partner chooses to end the union because your suspicions are unfounded and are damaging the relationship, you will need to take time to evaluate your behavior before you choose to get involved with another person.

If your partner has been dishonest with you, you will find that you still distrust your partner for an amount of time, but start acting as if you actually believe them and refrain from checking up on them. This is difficult as your instinct will be to protect yourself from future hurt, and the best way would be to monitor their activities. Practicing these actions of holding back your suspicion consistently will lead to changes in your behavior and eventually improvements in your relationship. If you do this for a long period of time, you will find that you can trust your partner and that it is okay. That nagging feeling at the back of your mind will begin to go away, allowing your relationship the room that it needs to grow.

In order for you to get to a place in your relationship where you fully believe your partner, you also need to make sure that you are operating from a space of integrity and are completely trustworthy. Your partner may be encouraged to mimic or reflect back to you your behavior. If for you trust means being open and honest with your partner, set the tone. Rather than asking for your partners social media account password, offer them yours. Instead of checking their phone constantly to tell whether they have lied to you, avail your phone so that they can do their own checks. Once your partner realizes how open you are to them and the relationship, they will reciprocate in a way that can only lead to your sustained satisfaction.

Tips for trusting in your partner

No matter what your reason is for not believing in your partner, what we discussed above is a great way to get started on the right track. The truth is though no matter what might have happened we all have trust issues, so chances are you and your partner both have times where you are silently or verbally question one another. What the two of you need to do is learn how to trust in each other.

One of the best ways to start trusting others is to first trust in yourself. In fact, trusting yourself is the very first step that anybody has to take when trying to solve any kind of trust issues. If you think about this it actually makes sense because if you don't trust yourself, you are never going to be able to trust another person.

Something else to think about when it comes to trusting in your partner is what exactly does trust mean. All too often trust issues are created because people have a different idea on what trust means. Not only do you each have different ideas on what trust means, you also have unique relationships. Since nothing is ever the same, you need to openly talk and communicate with your partner so you can discover together just what trust means in your relationship.

When it comes to trusting in your partner you are going to need to take a serious look at yourself first, and no we are not talking about trusting in yourself either. What you need to keep in mind when it comes to trust issues is that they often become a problem because it is some kind of issue you are secretly struggling with. For example, if you are worried about your partner cheating on you, it could be related to the fact that you have had thoughts about cheating in them. Finding out why you are having the trust issues can help you open up, but can also stop the crazy thoughts racing through your head.

Finally if you really want to work on building trust with your partner you are going to need to have an open relationship. By open we are talking about being honest with each other, no longer hiding any secrets, including trust issues you may have. Talk to each other about what is going on, the better your communication, the better chance you have at saving your relationship. And, don't forget that with trust you have to give it to receive it. Trust is not one sided, if you show a lack of trust in your partner, they are going to show a lack of trust in you. By trusting each other, you are going to quickly see your trust issues fading away.

Trust building exercises

As easy as believing in your partner might sound; it really isn't all that easy. This is especially true if trust issues have begun to plague your entire relationship. Once trust has been broken in a relationship it can be very hard to rebuild it. However, that doesn't mean it is impossible. Trust building exercises can be used to help rebuild trust once it has been broken, but they can also be used to make a good relationship stronger.

So, if you are ready to work on rebuilding that trust, here are some great trust building exercises you can try, so you can start believing in your partner once again.

Fall back

This is probably one of the oldest exercises around, as everybody has at least heard of it. It also happens to be one of the hardest exercises to carry out, even if you fully trust the person, if you are having relationship problems it is even worse. This exercise requires you to stand in front of your partner and simply fall back and trust them to catch you. In doing this exercise you have to trust in your partner enough not to look back at them while you are falling or even extend your arms out to catch yourself as you are going down. Once you are successful, do it again, but with a further distance between the two of you; if you can accomplish this, your relationship is defiantly worth saving.

Walking blindfolded

Walking blindfolded literally takes away your sense of sight, which you rely heavily upon to get you places. While you are blindfolded have your partner take you for a walk around a room that is filled with several obstacles. During this walk have them guide you through the room with a slight touch or even with verbal directions. As a variation you can have your partner take you for a walk outside as well.

In order to accomplish this walk you will have to have total trust in your partner, without it you and your partner will both fail at this exercise.

Filling in the blanks

This one is not just interesting, it is also very entertaining. To accomplish this exercise you are going to need two sheets of paper. On the first sheet you need to write down a few sentences about how you feel about your partner. On the second piece of paper write down these same sentences, but leave out the adjectives, verbs, and emotions. Have your partner fill in the blanks.

This exercise serves a few different purposes; it allows you to see what your partner really feels about you, but it also allows you to freely express your feelings about your partner. This exercise is also a great way to help improve communication between you and your partner, as you are able to express things that you might not otherwise say to your partner. Keep in mind this exercises isn't all about the positive comments, as you are going to come across some negative ones too. What you and your partner need to do in those cases is work on addressing the negative issues to help improve your relationship.

Eye contact

Many people don't often realize the importance of eye contact, it is vital for building trust in a relationship. Establishing good eye contact opens up communication between you and your partner, but it gives you insight as to what is really going on with your partner. With how important eye contact is in building trust and opening communication, it is amazing more couples don't know how to do it. If you and your partner need help establishing eye contact here is a great way to do it.

Start by standing face to face with your partner, maybe about a foot away from each other. Look directly into each other's eyes without smiling or making any kind of faces, for a period of 60 seconds. Once you are able to accomplish that, move closer together. At this point you want to be pretty close to touching and then repeat the exercise. Once you have accomplished that think about how you feel, focus on the intensity of the bond between the two of you at that point. Then move back until you are about 2 feet away from each other and repeat the exercise. Notice how the bond isn't nearly as strong at this distance; the feelings of trust are also lower at this distance.

When Your Partner Does Not Trust You

These exercises are excellent for building up trust when you need to trust your partner again. However, what do you do when your partner does not trust you? You may suggest that you take part in these exercises, though it is likely that you will be met with some reluctance.

Perhaps you did something that broke your partners trust, perhaps you did not do anything at all. In any case, you need to be able to build trust again. Here are some tips that should help you to get your partner to believe in you and your relationship.

Apologize

If you did something wrong, make sure that you being the recovery process for your relationship with a sincere apology. Take responsibility for your actions and avoid inclusion of any excuses that in any way justify what you had done wrong. Your intention by apologizing is not to minimize the seriousness of the issue, rather it is to make sure that you partner sees you are genuinely ready to make the right steps to improve your relationship. Real remorse points to someone realizing that they did something wrong and wanting to make it right.

Patience

Do not expect your partner to immediately get up and agree with your apology so that you simple move forward. Be aware that things are going to take some time to get back to normal, and to the place where your partner is able to believe in you again. The time that will take varies from one relationship to the next, and therefore, is completely out of your control. Do not push your partner for a rapid resolution as this may backfire on you, actually causing your partner to move further away from you rather than closer to you. It may appear to be a sign of disrespect which in no way helps your efforts.

Empathize

Put yourself in your partner's shoes and consider how you would react to a similar situation that affected trust. Can you blame your partner for having their reaction? You need to speak to your partner from a point of understanding, with an intention of showing them that you acknowledge the pain that they may be going through, and are willing to do what it takes to move past the pain and rebuild the relationship. Show them that you want to help with the process, and let them know that all they need to do is tell you how you can go about it.

Looking at these pointers is an assurance that handling the little things in a relationship will take you a long way in developing trust.

Chapter Four:
Comparing Yourself to Others

Self-esteem refers to the confidence in one's own worth or abilities. When a person has strong self-esteem they can confidently stand up for themselves and their beliefs. They are less likely to lose confidence in themselves because of another person's actions or words. However, self-esteem is delicate and can be easily shaken. It is often based on opinion instead of facts, and can be easily swayed by peer pressure. A person with low self-esteem or self-esteem issues is unable to trust their own judgment, may not feel secure in their own values and principles and worry excessively about what others think of them.

It's a well-known fact in the psychology industry that people who have self-esteem issues are constantly comparing themselves to other people. This behavior is actually quite natural for most people, though it does become a problem when you use the comparisons to put yourself down.

If you're a woman, comparison usually has to do with your figure, beauty and looks, superiority or inferiority, or being successful in a relationship. You assess the state of your body by looking at magazine models or other women in your vicinity and start to pick apart your features. Today, women are bombarded with information on what is expected to be ideal, perfect or preferred. At some point, it was very skinny women, then there was an appreciation for women with curves, and sometimes, the world is looking to embrace plus size women. These public opinions are fickle, and when one compares themselves to others they will often come short, or spend too much time trying to fit into what is the current trend rather than accepting themselves for who they are. This means that these women are constantly in a state of anxiety, apprehension and frustration, and it is these emotions that they carry with themselves into a relationship.

Men often compare each other when it comes to looks and success as well. They may believe that it is richer, more successful men that get the ladies, or that they need to have a buff body to be accepted. Therefore, they will compare themselves based on their pay checks, club memberships or the cars that they drive. They may try to be taller, have thicker hair, a smaller waistline and a more muscular frame to fit in with what society has dictated is the perfect man.

Striving for this perfection instead of self-acceptance will lead to the man constantly feeling under pressure, and they may release this pressure on their partners within the relationship.

Someone at the gym might have a larger bust or maybe a guy had larger muscles and can lift more, but comparing yourself to other people is not going to help you feel better about yourself or make your significant other like you more. It will however, bring your insecurities out in glaring light.

When you compare yourself to others, no matter if it's your best friend or some random person walking down the street, all you are doing is telling yourself you are not good enough, that you are not worth it. Comparing yourself to others only creates more trust issues, as it feeds into the jealousy, anxiety, and insecurities that you already have.

Comparing yourself to others is not healthy, for either you or your relationship. The lucky ones are the ones that only do it a few times a year, but chances are if you are reading this that doesn't apply to you. Once you start comparing yourself to others, you won't be able to stop; it is a self-destructive cycle that leaves you constantly feeling like you will never be good enough. The cycle continues because you are constantly on the lookout for somebody who you are better than, which simply drags out the process of you feeling bad about yourself.

What you need to keep in mind is that everybody is different; you have different strengths and weakness than your partner and everybody else for that matter. There is not one single person in this world who is perfect, so quit trying to find somebody who is, quit trying to see how you measure up to everybody else, and accept yourself for who you are.

Gaining control

One of the best things that you can do to help your relationship is to gain control over your constant desire to compare yourself to others. Like many other things in your relationship you are not going to be able to make any changes over night, it took you years to form the habit after all. In order to fully break yourself of the habit it is going to take several weeks, but every day there is work that must be done.

One of the most important things in breaking this habit is it to retrain your mind. Rather than focusing on the negative things, such as she has prettier clothes, you need to direct your mind towards the positive things. Such as how nice you look in your new clothes. Doing this every day is going to help a lot when it comes to getting yourself on the right path.

When it comes to gaining control over your destructive habit of comparing yourself to others, something your mother first taught you when you were little is going to come in handy. As a tot, your mother taught you about being kind to others. This is something that you need to put to use in your current situation because the way you treat others is how others are going to treat you. For example, if you are judging somebody based on their nice clothes, you are going to assume they are making judgments about your clothes. Be aware that when you judge somebody, what you are judging them on is probably a weakness you are struggling with. Once you stop judging others on their weakness, you will see an improvement in yours.

As I mentioned before, there is no such thing as a perfect person in this world. Even though there is no such thing as a perfect person, that doesn't mean that somebody out there isn't going to do some things better than you. A perfect example of this is celebrities. These successful people are often worshiped to the point that others feel they can never achieve what they have. Instead of trying to live up to what these people have accomplished work hard to achieve your own dreams and goals. Use them as mentors rather than comparing yourself to them. If you like a hair style or an outfit they are wearing, model your own after it rather than feeling like you can never look as good as them.

Another great way to gain control over your desire to compare yourself to others is to admit that you are not always going to come out on top. Even if you are great at something, chances are somebody out there, somewhere can do it better than you. This doesn't mean that you aren't good enough though, it is just a means to come to terms with the fact that you are not always going to be the best.

Many times people compare themselves to others that are worse off than they are in an attempt to make themselves feel better about themselves. This is just plain wrong and will only cause more trust issues in a relationship. If you are working on rebuilding your relationship and resolving any trust issues, you need to love yourself for who you are, not who you wish you were. The sooner you accept yourself, the sooner you will be able to believe that your partner truly loves you for you, not for what you have or don't have.

Master your own self appreciation

Consider this, there are people out there who are going to be better than you at almost everything, but there is one person who has chosen to love you. They may not be able to define why they love you, but there's some deep part down within you, whether you want to call it a soul or just a part of your being, and the person you are with chose you because of that part. They chose to come home to you every night and that has to count for something. Rather than put yourself down by focusing on all your perceived negative attributes when you compare yourself with others, you should take a moment to be thankful and appreciative for the person who picked you out of the crowd and called you their own.

So, the next time you find you are comparing yourself to other people, stop and assess why you feel that way. Is the person you are comparing yourself to better than you in any respect? You should appreciate your body and your mind so that you build yourself up. Do they appear to be happier? Remind yourself that the grass is not always greener on the other side. You may not know someone's entire story. Do they have something that you want? Whether it is great hair or a fabulous body, what they have is attainable if you put in some effort. Was there something in your past that made you feel inadequate? If there was, acknowledge it. Then move on from that situation and remind yourself that you are a different person than you were then, and no matter what happened, no one had the right to make you feel that way.

Recognize that you are in control of your self-worth, and you can change how you feel about other people when it comes to jealousy. There is a reason that you are who you are, that you have had your life experiences, met certain people along the way and have your own unique abilities and attributes. Once you see yourself through powerful eyes, you will begin to realize that you cannot be like any other person. You are unique and your own person. This may mean that other people do not like you, or they will put you down so that they can shake your self-worth. As an individual, you need to be strong in who you are, as you have no idea of what insecurities could lead other people to behave in a cruel fashion.

Take a deep breath and stop your negative emotions mid-thought, or evaluate them quickly and move on. When you dwell in the negative, the only thing that you can definitely accomplish is attracting more negative thoughts and subconsciously setting yourself up for negative situations coming your way. So if someone tells you that you are not good looking, instead of spending time worrying about your nose or your hair and wishing you could be like someone else, acknowledge that you are different, everyone has a preference and that it is ok you are not that person's choice.

If you're at a party and you see someone who is dressed nicer than you or maybe you feel he or she is getting more attention then you, introduce yourself to that person and get to know them. It is much better for you to be upfront and get to know them, than to stand in a corner at the back of a room wishing that they would acknowledge you. You might be surprised and make a new friend out of someone who you thought was far better than you or beyond your reach in terms of communication. Or you may be shocked to find that they also suffer from low self-esteem and may be comparing themselves to other people in the room. Until you place yourself in a person's space, you are unlikely to know and understand their chain of thought. Should you discover that you are the one with the higher self-esteem and understanding, you can then take the opportunity to help them, and yourself, by reassuring them about their true worth.

A good example of people whom others thought could never be loveable might include some of the presidents in the past who are well down on their list of attractive attributes, but they had women who stood by them and loved them. By all accounts, it would seem impossible that they would find true love, especially if you were to base the possibility on their outer appearance. Some may have been short, bald, overweight or even facially unattractive, but they were still able to find love and move forward with their lives. Had they been overly concerned about their outer appearance, they may have found it difficult to develop and stay within a relationship without experiencing heightened disappointment (of their features) and jealousy towards their spouse.

To stop yourself from comparisons with others that make you feel inadequate, redirect your focus to your partner, so that you help to build them up. The more confident your partner is in themselves, the better your relationship can become. Also, once your partner begins to experience the positive feelings that come with improved self esteem, they are likely to want to do the same for you, so you will find yourself in a situation where you do not need to compare yourself with other people because you are fully accepted as you are by someone you love. It also helps when you fully accept your partner, including all their real or perceived flaws, and you refrain from comparing them to other people. The more you compare your partner to others, you chip away at their self esteem, and in the end, you may find that you have been the cause for insecurity showing up in your relationship. Just as you are a unique being who deserves acceptance for who you are, so does your partner.

A good thing to do would be letting your partner know that they look beautiful or handsome for an occasion and making sure that they feel that you love them. They will feel love by your actions. You can do simple things like smiling at them, gentle touches or embraces, or even listening attentively when they speak to you. Showing your partner that you love them is something that you should do often, as it is little actions like these that help to build up the relationship. These actions are meant to instill trust, prevent jealousy and reduce anxiety. They are to help your partner see their self-worth through your eyes. However, try not to go overboard as this might come across as fake or manipulative and your partner may begin to question your motives.

It is important to remember that when you compare yourself to others, you mainly do so on the surface – and the surface can be highly distorted. Until you know a person intimately, you are unable to compare yourself to them effectively. Just because a person looks well put together on the outside, does not mean that just below the surface the story is the same. Many people can look amazing, successful and happy on the outside, yet the live miserable lives with issues including addiction problems, financial woes and so on. People can hide behind make up and touch ups, but accepting yourself as you are allows you to confidently reveal yourself, without trying to mask all your flaws so that others can accept you. Your acquaintances are more likely to trust you if they know who you truly are and you remain authentic to that person.

Being Compared to Another

You may become jealous and insecure, and develop trust issues when you have a partner that compares you to other people. It is already clear that when you compare yourself to others, you are actually doing yourself a disservice, and opening up door to a range of issues. Handling being compared against your will to other people is a whole other issue.

When in a relationship, it is highly likely that you partner had someone in their life before they met you. That person clearly had some attributes that your partner appreciated, and that is why they were together, and there were also some attributes that were not appreciated which possibly led to their break up. You must be sure that your partner has fully broken that bond, otherwise, you may end up constantly being compared to the other party. This will leave you insecure and questioning whether your partner would remain faithful to you if put in a situation with their former partner.

Before the green eyed monster rears its ugly head in your relationship and damages what you have managed to build this far, here is what you can do.

Be Confident

Develop some confidence in who you are, and love yourself for it. It does not matter where you are in the world. It is likely that there will always be someone out there who is better than you in one way or another. If you are confident, this will not phase you, and you will realize that your partner is lucky to have you in their lives.

Consider the abilities that you already have that highlight and accentuate who you are and what you stand for. The opinions of other people, especially if they are negative and are not adding value to your life should not form the basis of how you view yourself.

Being confident will protect you from being jealous of a person who may not even know that they are being compared to you. This attribute may also make you appear more attractive, this curbing the need to instill jealousy in you or damage your trust.

You are the Chosen One

It can be disheartening when your partner constantly compares you to a former flame, especially if you know that they are still in touch and possibly friendly with each other. In this case, you may believe that with the right set of circumstances, you will be betrayed, and you do not trust your partner to be able to resist such a temptation.

This thinking will drive you crazy, without actually helping you in any other way. It is therefore important that you dispel it from your mind as quickly as you can muster. Instead, focus on the thought that you are the chosen one. Your partner has chosen to be with you for a reason, and there must be something that is appreciated from you, more than the former flame.

You need to be open with your partner and let them know that the comparisons that are being made are hurting you and damaging the relationship. It is important that you set some boundaries so that your partner is aware that if they cross the line and do something that they should not with their previous partner, the relationship would be irrevocably damaged.

Accept what you Cannot Control

In every situation within a relationship, there is only so much that you can do to ensure that you have everything under control. One of the things that you cannot do is control the way another person things, feels and behaves. If your partner continues to compare you to their previous partner, you should accept that this is how they are and they are unlikely to change. You then need to ask yourself a question or two. Are you willing to keep wondering about what your partner is doing with their ex, and accept that something could happen? Are you alright with being in a situation where trust is an issue? Or would you rather say goodbye to the relationship so that you can have some peace of mind?

Whatever it is that you decide you need to be aware that there are some trust issues which you cannot resolve on your own and these are the issues where the behavior is coming from your partner.

If you found your partner behaving in a certain way, it is likely that the behavior will continue for a considerable time, and so you need to know which action you will take to keep you happy or build the relationship.

Chapter Five:
Be Prepared to Lose your Partner

This chapter is not about taking your partner for granted, trying to exist in their absence or mourning them because of an unexpected death. Nor is it about having no expectations of your partner and not setting your own boundaries. It is about being comfortable enough with yourself, that should your partner choose to leave you, your world would not fall apart.

It is vital to remember that when it comes to your emotions, you can only control your own. You are not responsible for or able to control the emotions of anyone else. In addition, another person does not have the power to control your emotions or your feelings. Therefore, you are also unable to control all the circumstances that could lead to your partner leaving your relationship.

When you are in a relationship, you need to set boundaries and have some that can be termed as "non-negotiable." Non-negotiable boundaries are issues within a relationship that you will not stand for, no matter what the reason is, and it is with these that you set all of your boundaries. Should your partner do something that falls within your non-negotiable list, no matter how much you may love them, you would be willing to lose them and the relationship.

These non-negotiable items may include physical or emotional abuse, infidelity, financial betrayal, irresponsibility and so on. They are negative actions that would make you extremely uncomfortable or distrustful in your relationship. If these were your actual non-negotiable items, it would mean that if you found out that your partner had a secret bank account where they had saved millions without telling you, which would be a case of financial betrayal. If that happened you would immediately end the relationship.

The previous chapters of this book have informed and equipped you with information on understanding and dealing with jealousy, anxiety, trust, and insecurity. Now that you're able to exercise not feeling jealous, anxious, or insecure about your relationship, you should also begin to feel comfortable with the thought of being alone.

Being alone in this instance simply means being able to spend time away from your partner without experiencing any negative emotions. It does not mean that you are so independent in your relationship that whether or not your partner is there, it does not make a difference. For some people, the idea of being alone with their thoughts at any time during the day or night makes them feel anxious and afraid. Remember, negative emotions stem from fear, so you have to learn to love yourself and be comfortable with the thought of being alone or spending time away from your partner when necessary.

Loving yourself also ties in with your self-esteem, which is how you view and feel about yourself as a whole. If you have strong self-esteem, then you should be able to function well without your partner. It is likely that even before you met your partner, you would have been well put together, so by committing to them, you are simply adding on to an already stable environment. Should your self-esteem be weak, your relationship is likely to suffer under the strain of your anxiety in the absence of your partner. This would be because you may have ended up in a situation where your partner is everything in your life. So every activity, every occasion, and every day you are with your partner. Therefore if you lose them, your state of confusion and misery could be palpable.

Some people actually feel like their partner is someone who will always make them feel like they are the center of attention, and when their attention-giver is taken away from them by someone else, even if it is brief and innocent, they become upset. When you have a loving partner, they are likely to dote on you so that you can feel and experience their love, and also because they want you to be happy.

Problems begin to set in when you take their efforts for granted and begin to expect their good behavior rather than appreciate it. When you reach this stage, you view your partner more like property rather than another unique person, and if you are one of these people, then you must stop this behavior immediately. This behavior is likely to stifle your partner, making them feel trapped or imprisoned within the relationship, and once a person feels trapped, they want to act on this be breaking free. Your partner deserves to be with someone who is complete, who can respect their need to associate with others, and who also trusts them enough to understand that they would not intentionally cause hurt. Although this would be an excellent scenario, it may be easier said than done.

Think of it this way: love needs a strong environment that harbors fearlessness, trust and honesty in order to thrive. You have to be strong for your partner and be comfortable with them talking to others, without fear that they will stray just because they are not constantly fawning over you. You also need your partner to be strong for you, rather than an insecure person who never wants to leave your side. It would be worse for your relationship if your partner was miserable while always holding your hand. Although you may have accomplished the goal of always having them with you, they may be unable to fully express the love that they feel for you.

Both you and your partner need to have a sense of independence in your relationship. Independence refers to being able to be an individual, even whilst in the relationship. Often mistaken for a situation where you allow your partner to do whatever they want, whenever they want, independence is more about mutual understanding and respect so that the two partners in the relationship can also have a little bit of their lives all to themselves. When you review your situation and find that you do all activities with your partner, or you are with them all the time, then you need to assess and determine ways that you can create some personal space.

The main reason for this is that you and your partner are two different people. You likely had different upbringings, grew up in different backgrounds and have unique experiences that shaped you into the people that you have become. For this reason, even though you may enjoy many activities together, there should be at least one of two which you would prefer to experience on your own or with a different group of people.

Absence makes the heart grow fonder, and some time apart may be what you need to revive your relationship, as well as to strengthen it. If you find that your imagination is getting the better of you when you are away from your partner, imagine the worst case scenario and then imagine that you are thriving in this scenario.

For example, your worst case scenario may be that your partner is unfaithful to you. You can imagine yourself reviving your relationship through love and understanding, as well as holding your partner accountable for their actions. Here, the point is not to picture your partner apologizing profusely or taking any other actions, it is just to look at what you would be doing in the situation.

You could also picture yourself devoting your time and energy to activities that give you joy and build your confidence, rather than sitting down and wallowing in misery because of your partners betrayal. Where feelings of hurt could have overwhelmed you, you are no longer afraid because you know that you are prepared to face this situation if it were ever to arise. You have figured out what you would do if your partner was to leave, and the situation becomes less desperate in your mind that previously.

Take up a pen and paper or just mentally check off ten things that would be positive about your life if your partner were to up and leave you. This list could include items like being able to devote more time to yourself, going back to school, meeting new people, rediscovering the world through your eyes only, moving to a new place and so on. Once you have created this list, you will not feel afraid when you see your partner talking with someone else.

You will be confident enough to realize when their conversation could be harmless, and secure enough in yourself, so that if it is not, you are still able to function. Your partner will not feel smothered by your constant need for attention, and will more likely consider ways that they can get *your* attention and connect with you on a deeper level.

This also ties in with how you train a person to treat you. Should your partner see that you trust them and appreciate them, though you give them space to be themselves and do their own activities, they are likely to respond by allowing you the same liberties within the relationship. When you trust your partner and are confident in your relationship, you create more opportunities for your partner to reinforce your trust and create more joy.

Giving each other the space you need

If you are having trust issues in the relationship, giving your partner the space they need is going to be quite a difficult task. Chances are when you give them space you tend to think of all of those "what ifs" that can drive a person crazy. However, if you want to keep your relationship and make your partner happy at the same time you are going to need to give them some space. The last thing you need in a relationship riddled with trust issues is your partner feeling like you are imprisoning them.

Giving space isn't going to be easy, but with some hard work it can be done by following these simple, yet effective steps.

Step One: Heed warning signs

Pay attention to the various warnings signs that are saying you need to back off a bit. If you are spending every waking moment with your partner, chances are you really need to back things off. Spending all of your time together tends to cause people to feel like they are suffocating in the relationship or other negative feelings.

Step Two: Check for codependency issues

In a relationship the last thing you want is one that has codependency issues. When codependency issues are present one partner or both is taking things way too seriously, to the point that one person is usually controlling the other for whatever reason. If codependency issues are present that doesn't mean the relationship is doomed, it simply means you might need to seek professional help to work everything out. Without professional help the codependency issues are only going to get worse.

Step Three: Talk about it

If you aren't open and honest with your partner about how you are feeling or if they aren't honest with you about what is going on, things will never be resolved. Sit down and have a heart to heart conversation with your partner. When starting the conversation focus on the positive aspects of your relationship before moving into the fact that you need to spend time apart as well. When talking you want to avoid the blame game, don't use "you" statements, always use "I" statements. When talking about the fact that you or your partner want some space make sure what either of you mean by space is thoroughly defined, this can help keep feelings of fear and anxiety in check.

Step Four: You need other people

It's silly to think that the only person you are going to need in your life is your partner. Thinking that way is honestly the quickest way to end just about any relationship. When talking with your partner, explain to them that both of you need to spend time together with friends without each other. It's easier to tackle same-sex friendship before you address opposite sex friendships. Spending time apart with friends is all about trust, you have to show your partner that you trust them if you want the relationship to stay alive.

Step Five: You are soul mates

Chances are both parties in the relationship have some fears, no matter how deep down they might be buried. You and your partner need to focus on reassuring each other that you are committed to each other and that you are committed to the relationship. Just because you need some space doesn't change that act, it is simply going to make your relationship that much stronger, as long as the two of you work together.

Step Six: Pursue your interests

Before you and your partner got together, you each had your own set of interests. Those interests probably haven't changed, but they might have been pushed aside to enable your relationship to grow. To help spend some time apart to give each other the space you both need, both of you should consider praising your old interests.

Step Seven: Do things apart even when you are together

This one sounds a bit weird, but it is actually fairly straight forward. As you go out in social settings you and your partner need to act like you are not partners. Even though you are doing something together as a couple, you can still do things separately. For example, at a dinner party sit away from each other and engage in conversations with other. At a party, tell each other good-bye at the door and mingle with others, while occasionally

Step eight: Reassurance

No matter what kind of issues you might be dealing with, both you and your partner are going to need reassurance as you spend time apart. In terms of reassurance I am not just talking about saying everything is going to be fine. In this case, reassurance means that if you or your partner is concerned about too much distance or still not enough that you will come to one another and talk things out and then make the appropriate changes. And, regular good old reassurance that you love them and this space is not permanent space, is also a good idea.

Your Partner Will Not Let Go

You may have reached the point where you are prepared to leave your partner and have managed to get some independence. After evaluating the situation in your relationship, you realize that the trust issues are too great to overcome, and you make the decision to leave the relationships. You may then meet with a brick wall, and that is your partner refusing you to leave them.

Trust is interesting in relationships and can play on psychology in a fascinating way. Often times the partner that is guilty of wrongdoing will be the first to blame the other party for exactly the same, knowing full well that they are innocent. The partner that is innocent then goes into overdrive trying to reestablish trust and build the relationship, in essence working to prove that they are innocent and willing to love.

On the other end, the partner that has the issue continues with their wrong doing freely, knowing full well that they can manipulate their partner. This issues with trust, and the exploitation of another person's trust culminate into a situation that can best be described as being abusive.

When the person on the receiving end realizes that there is nothing that they can do to please their partner and gain the trust (which they had not done anything to lose in the first place), the decision may be made to leave the relationship. Should you find yourself in this situation there are several obstacles that you may face.

To begin with, your partner may refuse you to leave, because they know deep down that they are in the wrong, and that you have always been the innocent party. At this juncture, you have a few options. The first is to let your partner know that they need to earn your trust if they expect you to remain in the relationship, and the other is to get as far away from them as possible, despite what guilt and fear that they may try to impart on you.

If you are in a situation that has turned abusive, your partner may believe that you are leaving them for another person and risk harming you. Even the knowledge that you have done no wrongdoing will not help, as they view trust from their perspective, knowing that they are not trustworthy. If this is the situation that you are facing, you should leave the relationship carefully as there is every possibility that you partner may harm you for even considering bringing an end to the union.

It is a great challenge to establish trust in a relationship where one party wants to possess the other or finds fault and lays down accusations, even when there is no reason or basis to do so. The best thing would be to end the relationship and move forward.

Chapter Six:
Stop Playing Games

Due to the closeness that you have with another person when in an intimate relationship, it is very easy to have your feelings hurt. This is because you have often invested so much into the union that your lives have blended into each other. You feel as though your partner should be able to understand you, especially your emotions and reactions to situations. You also have expectations that they are meant to fulfill, and should they fall short, you are likely to be extremely disappointed. When something does not go your way in this setting, you may be tempted to start playing games.

In order for you to start with games, there needs to be some fundamental issues within your relationship. Perhaps you are having problems with communication, so that when you are unable to discuss your feelings openly and honestly with your partner. You may also have problems with trust, where they had exhibited similar behavior in the past, you had discussed and moved past it, and they it is showing up again. Or you may have grown up in an environment where people managed problems in their relationships by playing games, so those are the tools you have been equipped with. In any case, before you start playing games, you need some prompting behavior.

Take for example you've just caught your boyfriend in behavior that seemed like flirting while the two of you were at the bar or vice versa. This can be particularly annoying, especially if you have mentioned that you do not like this behavior to him before. You then believe that he does not take you seriously or care enough to stop. Now you're jealousy meter has blown past its maximum and through the roof. So what are you going to do about it?

69

As you have had your feelings hurt, you may intend for your partner to experience the same feeling, if possible with greater intensity than what you went through. You want them to hurt, so that they know how you feel and also so that they will never repeat the offending behaviour. Therefore your first reaction might be to do exactly what they are doing to you, which is to find a man or a woman and begin flirting with them right in front of your partner to get your point across that you're upset. While doing this you will give your partner sideways glances, and appear to be thoroughly enjoying yourself, just so that you can make sure that you see them being affected by your behavior.

Or you want to make your partner feel low for their behavior, so you even go to the extent of getting others to point out your behavior to your partner. You use shame as your game, and go out to make sure everyone knows how they have disappointed you with dishonesty and betrayed you within the relationship. However, this kind of behavior does you no good in the end.

At this juncture, it is important to assess your feelings and determine whether your reaction is excessive, and whether you fully understand what you think you saw. The mind is dangerous, as it can interpret a situation to highlight what you would like to see, rather than what is really there. Like you would in a legal case, the accused should be completely innocent until proven guilty. Usually, you will start to play games due to your interpretation of the situation rather than because you have hard and true evidence of misbehavior on your partners part.

The expected result you hope for may be a realization that you have been hurt, and a possible apology from your partner so that you can get back to the business of being a loving couple. This does not usually happen if your approach is playing games. Playing games only leads to mistrust, along with heartache and anxiety. Games threaten the very foundation of a relationship. In the end, two people are left feeling confused and hurt over what just happened, and the innocent bystanders are left feeling, well, used. If you don't care that your partner feels hurt and upset, then think about what you've just done to yourself.

Although playing games are meant to elicit some response from the person that hurt you, they often entail you giving something up in order to get your point across. You have lost your dignity in front of other persons. You've just looked desperate, insecure, and foolish in front of others because you got a little jealous about innocent, or even not innocent, flirting. You have opened yourself up to judgment, and this can be either fair or unfair.

Instead of exploring playing games as an option, you should focus on ways that you can improve the other issues in your relationship. The most important one in this situation is open and honest communication. This is the type of communication that is factual, non-critical and expressive. It is where you explain your issues and expectations, without needing your partner to react in a particular way.

If you have a serious problem about what just occurred with your partner, find a quiet place at the bar or even wait until the two of you are home and tell them in a calm, polite way about how you feel. By communicating honestly, openly and privately, there is a better chance that your partner will realize the error of their ways and want to consciously make an effort to help you feel better about the situation.

Try starting with this sentence: "I feel upset because you..." and finish it. Don't use expletives or raise your voice, but make sure that your partner understands what they did to make you feel bad. If they care about you, they will talk to you about what happened and the two of you will work things out. They may also become defensive and react with an outburst or frustration. As long as you have done your best to communicate with them effectively, a negative reaction should not affect you. Give your partner time, and they will surely think about their reaction and find a way to come and address the situation with you. Remember, you are an adult and acting out on jealousy by choosing to play games is not an adult action.

The danger for playing games with the relationship is heightened when you are using the results of those games as relationship ammunition if something were to occur in the future. This basically means that whether you are the one playing games, or the one suffering as a result of game playing, rather than confronting the hurt that has been created you're your partner, you simply store away this information. This is akin to building up a wall in your relationship, where every piece of information that you keep is one brick. Once the wall is up, it is impossible for your partner to see the other side unless they climb above it or break through it. It separates you from each other. If you have been storing away information due to your game playing, when you are in the midst of an argument, you blow up and use as much information from the game playing as possible to hurt your partner. Your partner is likely to feel betrayed that you had been harboring all those thoughts without addressing them reasonably, and also angry that you have chosen to use them against your partner, especially in anger. When upset, they are likely to be exaggerated and if it is something that your partner feels shame about, they may find it difficult to forgive that this information has been brought up.

To save your relationship, and build trust, you should avoid playing games completely – not sometimes, not based on any situations, but completely. Playing games can sometimes happen as a result of putting your trust in other people. For example, you may speak to a trusted friend or family member about a problem within your relationship. They could recommend that you go about the problem in a roundabout way so as to test your partners love or devotion to you. When you are in the midst of the game, you may feel as though you have lost and dug yourself into a whole that you cannot get out of. You could lose your relationship entirely.

Instead of making you look bad in front of others and lowering your self-esteem, walk away from the situation or talk about your problems or concerns in an adult manner at home or in a private area. Do not make your problems public by sharing them with people who love you so much, they will always be biased towards you and may offer you bad advice, simply because they want what is best for you. If your partner seems to think that your emotions do not matter, perhaps it is time to look for someone else or reevaluate how you are behaving. A partner who loves you and is determined to have a relationship work with you will make sure that they do not indulge in game playing, and that you both benefit from your relationship with each other.

If you are not the one who is playing games, but rather are dealing with a partner who is playing games, your best bet is to attempt to communicate with them about the games and how they make you feel. You will have to push for open and honest behavior in your relationship. If that is the only way that your partner knows how to behave within a relationship, you can begin to develop trust and reduce anxiety by reviewing your behavior. Be sensitive to the things that make your partner anxious and concerned, and avoid behaving in any way that brings out the worst in them. It may seem unfair, or as though you have to change yourself in order to be in the relationship. You should view changing your behavior as a compromise in this instance, so that you can stop your partner from sabotaging the relationship and develop a positive way to move forward.

Improving your communication

Playing games in a relationship simply adds to the trust issues that are already there. Instead of playing games you need to work on improving your communication. The problem with communication in any kind of relationship is two people with two different opinions are coming together, so what you might think in regards to open and honest communication is different than what your partner might think.

One of the biggest misconceptions with communication is just because you are talking to one another you are communication. Talking is a form of communication, but what you talk about determines the level of communication going on. A surface topic, such as how your day was or how the kids are doing, is talking not really communicating. Communicating is talking openly about the important stuff and the better your communication the stronger your relationship will be.

Here are several ways that you can help eliminate trust issues in your relationship by improving your communication.

Stop what you are doing and listen

Honestly, this is in just about every article or book you will ever read in regards to improving communication. And, while it might sound like something simple and easy to do, it is actually a lot harder than you think. When talking with your partner, especially when it something important, it is hard to stop what you are doing and listen to what they have to say. You don't want to let go of your thoughts or opinions because you are worried that your partner won't listen to what you have to say. In your rush to talk over each other, communication is lacking. You need to really stop and listen to what each other has to say to ensure both of you are heard.

Really listen

This is another piece of advice that is common in communication books, but it is also a good one. Even though you might have stopped talking that doesn't mean you are actually listening to your partner. Chances are you are still thinking about stuff you want to say in response to something your partner has already said. Reflection is one of the best ways to ensure you are actually listening. Reflection involves rephrasing what your partner has said to ensure you understood them. However, if not done carefully it can come across as mocking or rude, so be sure to use it sparingly and always explain to your partner why you are doing it.

Honesty

Now for some this is going to be hard because they have never learned how to be open and honest with others. However, if you want to have great communication in relationship you need to be entirely open and honest with each other, which includes your needs and desires. You cannot hide your emotions, hiding them is similar to lying and lying is never good in a relationship, no matter how small or insignificant the lie is. Being open and honest means no giving your partner the silent treatment or pretending everything is okay when it's really not. If you are being open and honest with your partner you will talk to them about everything, including things you have never told anyone else. Being open and honest often means making yourself vulnerable, but that is the only way you are going to realize the full potential of your relationship.

Nonverbal signs

When it comes to communicating with each other nonverbal signs are just as important as the words you are saying. How you say something plays a big role in how your partner receives it. So, when talking to one another pay attention to the nonverbal signs to aid you in communicating better. Nonverbal signs include body language, tone of voice, eye contact, as well as your voice's inflection and how far or close you are to one another. To improve communication you need to improve how well you can pick up on the nonverbal signs. For the best communication you have to be able to read your partners nonverbal signs, while always being aware of your own.

Stay focused

Sometimes when you are talking to one another and feelings start to run a little high, the conversation can get a bit heated. If that is the case, the conversations tend to veer off in different directions. To improve communication skills you will want to work on keeping the conversation focused on the subject. No matter how tempting it might be, avoid taking any kind of cheap shots at your partner as it is not going to help matter at all. If the discussion veers off it usually makes the situation worse, so do your best to get it back on track.

Just like most things in a relationship communication is not going to get better overnight. If you and your partner are serious about improving your communication, it is something that you are going to have to consciously work at. However, the more you work at it the easier it will become and before you know it you will be able to be entirely open and honest with your partner about everything, which will go a long way towards resolving any trust issues in the relationship.

Chapter Seven:
Stop Your Overactive Imagination

Take a deep breath and relax. This chapter will begin with an exercise for your mind. Picture in your mind that you are preparing for Valentine's Day at a beach resort. You can see the soft sand, the sun is warmly shining down, and you are wearing something that is blowing softly in the wind. You are holding hands with your sweetheart and walking towards the pier for a romantic dinner. Hold the picture in your mind for a moment and then release it.

It is quite possible that when you were putting together the picture, you added in elements that were not described here. You possibly added some water and waves, because the description said you were at the beach. Your dinner table may have had candles because it was described as being romantic. And the color red may have featured somewhere by virtue of the fact that you were there for Valentine's Day. This is just an example of how the imagination works to create a scenario or paint a picture. It is able to use your existing knowledge to make inferences and clarify a description.

The mind is extremely powerful when it comes to making assumptions and creating scenarios. In fact, you have possibly experienced your mind "running away" with your thoughts. This is what occurs when you start off with one little thought, and before you know it, you have created several chapters of a tantalizing story that usually ends in tragedy. When it comes to negative thinking, the mind runs away with excessive speed in comparison to positive thinking, and all this is because you allow your imagination to be overactive.

The Valentine's Day description above is a normal example of using the imagination. It becomes overactive when you go beyond the parameters mentioned and start picturing yourself with children two years down the road because of that one day. It is the overactive use of the imagination that fuels psychological problems in people. They're unable to differentiate between reality and their imagination.

This is what happens to people who are experiencing jealousy, anxiety, and insecurity. This can make the normally sane individual appear to be crazy, or they may behave in a crazy and irrational manner. While the imagination can be a powerful, awesome tool, it can also instill unnecessary fear in us, affecting our trust in relationships and creating a base for anxiety. As an individual, you must learn ways that you can control your imagination.

Therefore, you need to stop trusting your imagination because it is not always right. Imagination is different from intuition. Intuition is a gut feeling whereas imagination is a picture in your mind. You can trust your gut feelings more than the picture. You should learn how to consciously evaluate your feelings, and base all your reactions on solid facts rather than suppositions.

Here's a scenario to better explain what I mean:

Your significant other is late from work and you're beginning to worry. You're checking the clock more and more often and they're not responding to their texts. You have tried to call them repeatedly and they are not picking your calls, or your calls are going straight to voicemail. When they don't respond, your initial emotion is concern, and you hope that they are ok and have not come to any harm.

However, as time changes so does your disposition and you imagine that they're at the bar with their coworker and they're both getting pretty drunk. After all, you know that your partner enjoys a cold glass of white wine after a long day's work, and their coworker is attractive, so the combination of the wine and the attractive coworker could be the beginning of an affair. You remember how you were once at the office and you spotted the coworker staring at your partner. Was that unusual interest that you saw in their eyes?

As time passes by, even if it's just a few minutes and it's impossible for what your mind has come up with to happen in that timeframe, you imagine that they're at a hotel room and they're doing the horizontal tango. In fact logically, you believe they downed those glasses of white wine at the bar so that they could rush off for their secret tryst. So vivid is the picture in your mind that you almost feel as if you are in the room and watching them at it live.

You've now become angry, frightened, and upset without having any evidence that your partner is doing any of those things. You are full of jealousy and anxiety and may even begin to hyper ventilate. However, the more you think about them together, the more plausible they seem. The scenario becomes a part of your reality, and if anyone was to speak to you at that moment, you would tell them with all surety that your partner is being unfaithful. More time seems to be passing. You're texts might be becoming more frequent and you even try to call them and you are still getting no response. You begin to feel desperate and as though your world is falling apart. You need reassurance and advice so that you do not go completely crazy.

At this juncture, you are so emotionally distraught that you call a friend and tell them all about how your partner is being unfaithful. In tears, you explain that you believe your partner is having an affair with their co-worker. You describe in detail how they probably had a drink after work to let off some steam and then most likely headed off to a hotel together. Your friend, who tries to be supportive, tells you that you need to confront your partner with this information, and get them to explain why they would betray you in this way. There may also be a suggestion that you should demand an apology from your partner, or in the worst case, consider leaving your relationship. At this point, not only has you painted a picture in your mind of your partners behavior, you have also started to seek advice on how you can justify your next course of action.

This is where your mind should begin to consider other scenarios, rather than your overactive imagination feeding into a paranoid delusion. What you may have forgotten is that they might be on the road and they can't respond or they're in a late meeting that was last minute and completely out of their control. Maybe he's stopping at the grocery store to pick up flowers for you because he knows that he is late and wants to make it up to you.

By the time your partner gets home, you are so het up that any communication that they attempt will simply fly past you. In your mind you may be thinking, how dare they? Why does my partner think I am so stupid? How could my partner betray me like this? You decide that the best thing you can do to handle the situation is to give him or her the silent treatment and being very cold and abrasive over something that happened in your mind. In contrast, you may begin an argument and air out all your worries and opinions, which if unfounded will greatly offend and anger your partner which could make the situation much worse than it should be.

The truth of the situation is that what you just imagined is not reality, and even if it was, you have no proof or evidence that should have made you feel that way. Your mind was simply playing on your insecurities, and you happily allowed your thoughts to "runaway" with you.

With this undercurrent of mistrust, the situation will inevitably lead to a fight between you and your partner, and that's not going to solve anything. Therefore when you find yourself in this situation where you are wondering where your partner could be, rather than allowing your imagination to run away with you into the negative, you could choose to build your relationship by using your imagination in a positive way.

So, when you make that phone call to your friend seeking assurance and a loving ear, you should instead ask for advice on what you can do to make your partner happier once they arrive home. Explain that they have been working hard and you feel the need to reward them in some way. This way, your friend can be a positive influence in your life and relationship, instead of being the scape goat that you go to during moments of emotional distress.

Create a romantic dinner or setting as you wait for your partner. Take time to light up candles and play soft music to set the mood. Cook a special dinner or choose a romantic movie you know they would like so that you have an excuse to cuddle up to them after their long day. Work on creating a peaceful situation or atmosphere, and trust that they love you enough to always be honest with you.

By using your imagination more positively, you are unlikely to feel debilitating anxiety and stress. It also allows you enough time to calm you mind and address any issues or concerns in the right way with your partner. Arguments and fights are avoided and your partner is likely to appreciate you and your temperament more.

Controlling your imagination requires a conscious effort from you, to monitor your thoughts and stop them when they begin to veer towards the negative. The great thing is, although challenging at first, once you have mastered this ability, it will remain and positively affect every aspect of your relationship.

Quieting Your Mind

Sometimes as your imagination takes off it can be very difficult to turn it off, no matter how hard you might be trying. If you ever catch your imagination running wild what you need to do is immediately quiet your mind. In order to quiet your mind you are going to need to let the thoughts flow through your mind, but you cannot pay them any kind of attention. Giving them attention is allowing them to take root, which makes it harder to quiet those horrible thoughts.

Quieting your mind is not going to be easy, but once you master this it is well worth it. Here are some tips that you can easily to put to use so you can master quieting your mind.

Everything passes

No matter how hard things get, you need to remember that everything is going to pass. So, as your imagination starts to run wild, your anxiety is probably going to go through the roof, so what you need to do is remind yourself that it will pass. How you do this will vary on what works best for you, but many people find asking themselves questions about what they are going to take away from this lesson and how it will help them become a better person. Sometimes journaling it works even better.

Use a recording

Picturing yourself sometime in the future, how far into the future is your choice; you will want to record yourself speaking to yourself. When talking to yourself give yourself some words of encouragement. Talk about how to handle various problems, including any anxiety attacks you might be having. You can even talk about some of your insecurities and a way that you have found to deal with them. Basically, you are going to want to create a recording telling yourself that everything is going to be fine, no matter what you are currently thinking. Play back the recording as often as you need to help calm your thoughts.

Allow it to happen

When you are dealing with anxiety, sometimes trying to handle the problem is worse than letting everything just play out. So, if you are imaging a worst case scenario in your head, let it just play out, as trying to put a stop to the thoughts can cause you to fly into an even worse panic. As your anxiety attack plays itself out, look at what is going on and ask yourself if worrying is going to do any good. If worrying isn't going to help, allow yourself to move on. The key here is to not beat yourself over having negative thoughts, but to redirect your thoughts to the positive outcome of it.

Picture how you want it to be

Part of quieting your mind is to use your imagination, but you want to use it in a constructive way. Play out how you want things to happen inside your head, even if you can't make the changes now to your current situation, it can help keep your thoughts from going out of control. The more worried you are the more help visualizing a positive outcome will be because your brain doesn't know it isn't real and will release the hormones needed to calm yourself down.

Distractions

If you are overly worried about something try to distract yourself. How you distract yourself will depend on what you enjoy doing, but you want to find something that is going to allow you to totally immerse yourself. Getting distracted allows you to refocus your thoughts, which helps calm the noise inside your head.

Be thankful

When you let your imaginations run wild you tend to get stuck in a whirlwind of negative thoughts and emotions. What you need to do is refocus those thoughts and feelings to help calm the turmoil within. One way to do that is to think about the stuff that you are thankful for. By doing this you quickly realize just how much you have to be thankful for, which helps calm your thoughts almost instantly because you realize it could always be worse.

What you need to remember, even as your imagination is running rampant, is that no matter how much you might want to you cannot control those around, especially not your partner. You have the choice to allow your imagination to drive you crazy or you can simply work towards quieting your mind each time things get out of hand.

Chapter Eight:
Letting Go

When you met your partner, they were free as a bird, and likely it is in that freedom that you found them most attractive. They were able to express themselves fully, show you into their world and love openly without fear of judgment. Just as you saw positive attributes in them, they also saw positive attributes in you. Together, you made the decision to commit to each other and explore a relationship.

At the beginning of your relationship, you probably spent all your time together trying to learn as much as you could about each other. Every day was an adventure and brought something new. You enjoyed each other's company so much, you could not imagine being apart, you were deeply reassured that your partner wanted to be with you always. The moment that they made a commitment to be with you, your insecurities set in and you possibly felt the need to keep them on a leash of sorts to stop them from straying too far away from your loving clutches.

This is where controlling behavior sets in. This behavior may include your need to know where they are at all times, needing information on how they spend their money, judging and choosing their friends for them. It may even go as far as you choosing their clothing, so that you make sure they do not appear to be too attractive in the eyes of others. Controlling, though misguided, comes from a basis of love and desire. The only issue that it is love surrounded by mistrust and anxiety.

Basically, controlling behavior slowly chips away at your partner's personality, and changes them into what you believe is your ideal partner. It strips them of who they truly are. If you are the person at the receiving end of controlling behavior, you are likely to harbor a lot of resentment towards your partner, fundamentally changing the makeup of your relationship. Whether expressed or not, resentment that is building below the surface will eventually come out in a fit of anger.

Now that you're able to understand why your imagination is going overboard and you short circuit that train of thought, relax your possessiveness and control over your partner. In the same way that they do not own you, and should not be able to control your every move, you should not believe that you own them.

Your partner is a unique individual with their own feelings, desires, and behavior. You should accept them for who they are rather than trying to get them to fit a mold of what you expect. There is clearly something that they loved about you, and that is why they chose to be with you rather than all the other women or men available. This should give you confidence in your partner, instead of having you question their sanity at choosing to be with you.

Whether you see it as being possessive or not, your partner and others will see your jealous behavior as just that. If they choose to look a little deeper, they may even begin to have pity on you, as they will see the insecure, scared, and easily intimidated person lurking just beneath the surface. Your partner may feel objectified rather than appreciated for who they really are. This may mean that they feel disconnected from you emotionally, and therefore will begin to distance themselves slowly from you.

When you are possessive, your partner's friends and family are likely to discourage them from developing a deep relationship with you. They may say phrases like "your partner is trying to trap you", or "why does your partner behave in such an insecure way", or even "your partner is trying to take you away from those you love." Rather than support, you will receive opposition and your relationship will become an uphill battle.

This can spell disaster in the relationship as you must take into consideration that your partner has been connected with family much longer than they have been connected with you. They are more likely to give in to pressure from family and end the relationship, especially if within the relationship they are not feeling entirely comfortable, loved, and accepted for whom they really are.

For your partner, this type of behavior from you can be embarrassing and stifling, and it may lead them to leave you in the end anyway. They may feel that there is no trust and no matter what they do, they cannot overcome your jealousy or insecurity.

If they choose to stay with you, they may decide to be unfaithful, simply because you are trying to block all avenues of their communication with the outside world. When someone feels stifled or trapped, they usually try their very best to escape.

Therefore, it is safer to lengthen the leash and allow your partner to spend the weekend with their friends or chat with their attractive colleague at a business lunch or on holiday party. In fact, you should encourage them to develop friendships and interests outside of your relationship, so that you can create a balance and also, so they do not lose their personal identity. When you partner is able to be themselves, they are able to offer you the best of themselves, and the same applies to you as well.

By trusting them, they can then behave in a way that is trustworthy. You are able to hold them accountable for their actions, and if they really prove that they cannot be trusted, you can then make an informed decision on the future of your relationship.

If your partner feels stifled, he or she may also feel justified to act out in an attempt to regain their freedom. And, they will do so holding you solely responsible for their behavior.

Examples of this can be seen in many areas, where people make statements like, "I had an affair because my partner did not love me well," or "my partner does not understand me so I had no choice but to stray." It is a sad state of affairs, but very possible.

Keep in mind that your partner may not find the person they're talking to as attractive as you perceive them to be. As you are unable to put yourself into your partner's heart, soul, and mind to know first-hand what they are thinking and feeling, you should refrain from making assumptions about their behavior. In addition, you should avoid reading too much information into the situation, especially if it could be explained innocently. When looking at this scenario, you should also consider body language as we communicate more without words than with them.

You are quite likely to view the person they are speaking to through your own insecurities, rather than through the attributes that you perceive your partner finds attractive. You're are probably worrying about nothing and creating a situation or problem where there is none. Instead of worrying about your partner's thoughts, you should take time to discuss your insecurities, and this then empowers your partner to reassure you of your standing in their lives.

Discussing your insecurities will require you to be vulnerable, and should move your relationship to a deeper level. Once you have been yourself freely and honestly, should your partner choose to end the relationship, you should be able to let go and move forward knowing that you gave yourself 100% to the union, and there is nothing more that you could have done.

If you do not do these things, your partner is going to feel as if they are being cut off from their world. They may feel separated from their family and friends, and deeply hurt because of this. At the extreme end, they may even feel completely isolated and possibly emotionally abused.

Imagine if someone tried to put you in a cage or on a leash and control your every move. You would be angry, afraid, and upset. Escape would be the top item on your agenda. Your partner feels the same way. You should invest your time in treating your partner exactly the way you would like to be treated.

That brings forward to another point, empathy.

Empathy is being able to understand how another human being feels. It means that you can put yourself in their shoes and view a situation through their eyes. Always try to think about why someone is acting or reacting the way they are and look at it from their viewpoint. You might need to take into consideration their past experiences, and they way that there were handled.

If you decide that you would not like someone treating you the way you are treating them, perhaps it's time to change your behavior.

Dealing with your insecurities

Struggling with jealousy, is often related to the fact that you are struggling with your own insecurities. Regardless of what your insecurities are or how they developed as we mentioned before, they are going to wreak havoc in your current relationship. The more insecure you are, the tighter your hold is on your partner. If you have any kind of hope in making this relationship work, despite the trust issues going on, you are going to need to deal with all of your insecurities head on, you must stop running from them.

I won't ever lie to you; dealing with your insecurities is not going to be easy. In fact, it is most likely going to be one of the hardest things that you have ever done because you are going to have to look deep inside yourself and your past to come to terms with the things that have happened. Despite it not being easy, it is something that can be done; you just need to know where to get started.

Here are some of tips that you will find useful when it comes to dealing with your insecurities.

Attitude

I cannot stress enough just how important your attitude is, it literally affects every aspect of your life. Due to your numerous insecurities you have probably developed what we term a "what if" attitude. This kind of attitude has you constantly second guessing what is going to happen next. With a "what if" attitude you are constantly thinking in terms of the worst case scenarios, based on whether scenario A happens or scenario B does. I will be honest with you; this attitude will literally drive you insane, as well as push your partner as far away as possible. You need to shake off the "what if" attitude, and the best way to do that is to train yourself to tell yourself so what whenever you start doing the "what if" game.

Awareness

In order to change anything, we must first be aware of the issues, denying that there is a problem is only going to make things worse. If you really want to deal with your insecurities head on, you are going to have to figure out what they are, as well as what is triggering them. Are you insecurities related to a person being prettier than you or perhaps somebody who can sing, whereas you can't; No matter what they are, once you figure out what makes you insecure, you can figure out what you can do to successfully deal with them.

Figure out your fears

One thing that many people find out about their insecurities is that they are directly linked to their fears. So, in order to overcome your insecurities, you are going to have to first tackle your fears. Your best bet is to create a list of all of your fears, even if it seems trivial, jot it down. Once you know what your fears are, you can work on overcoming them by figuring out what methods will work best in tackling your fears. Every time you tackle a new fear, your self-confidence is going to grow.

Journal

Insecurities play such a huge role in your life because of how much attention you give them. The more you focus on them, the more likely they are to bring you down. To help keep your attitude positive, you want to focus on areas where you have succeeded in overcoming your fears, not just on how to overcome them. A great way to start focusing on the positive side of things is to create a journal. Fill your journal with times of where you have succeeded in something, whether it was a goal you set for yourself or a fear you have finally overcome. Then on the days where you are really struggling you can go back to your journal and read something positive.

Goals

One of the biggest culprits behind your insecurities, is your lack of goals. If you don't have goals or enough goals set out for yourself, you are going to wander through life, often feeling lost and alone. Not knowing what you are supposed to be doing is enough to make you feel like you are going nowhere in life. Instead of allowing that to happen, work on setting some goals for yourself. These don't have to be some kind of outrageous goals; you just want to make sure the ones you are setting are ones you can actually achieve. The more goals you achieve, the better you are going to feel about yourself, giving you a better sense of self-worth.

Laughter

There is the saying that laughter is the best medicine. You might be surprised to learn that there is some truth to that. Several studies have shown that laughter is a great way to help improve the mood. If you think about it, it actually makes sense because if you are laughing about something it is hard to be mad or angry. Friends are an excellent way to get you laughing, but you can also achieve this on your own. When you are feeling insecure about something or find yourself playing the "what if" game, go find something funny to watch or even read.

Friends

Along with laughter, friends are also a great way to help you feel better about yourself, but they must be true friends, not just acquaintances. Many times simply the cat of sitting down with a close friend when you are feeling insecure is enough to make you feel better, especially as they allow you to vent freely about everything going on. When venting to a friend, you get the feelings off your chest, but your friends are also a great way at pointing out just how good of a person you really are. A lot of times dealing with insecurities, is more about focusing on the positive rather than dwelling on the negative. Good friends not only do that, they cheer you up when you are feeling down, and we all know just how much a good laugh does in terms of lightening up the mood.

One thing that you need to bear in mind is that letting go has many different meanings. If you are tired of letting your jealousy, anxiety, and insecurities control your every move it's time to let them go. Hanging onto your insecurities is only going to lead to one thing, which is the end of your relationship. To start resolving trust issues you have to tackle your insecurities head on, if you don't it will most likely lead to you having to let go of your relationship.

Chapter Nine:
Imagining a Positive, Self-Confident You

By this juncture, you have an idea of how powerful your mind is and the effects that your thoughts can have on your relationship. Your thoughts are extremely powerful, and philosophers have long said that what you think is what you become. So, then you can use your imagination to build your self-confidence if you have been suffering from insecurity and jealousy. Using your imagination can bring forth a situation that you wished for but that does not yet clearly exist.

Remember how your imagination went wild when your partner was fifteen minutes late getting home? Well, now is the time to turn that imagination around for the better and use it to make yourself feel more confident and positive about you.

For example, you are with your partner in a public place and you see a famous person that your partner admires. You can see them get excited, a smile breaks out on their face and they are eagerly heading in that direction to get a photograph. If you have low self-confidence, you will tell yourself that they are only doing that so that they can compare you with the famous person. You may also think that they like the famous person more than you, which is why they want to get the photograph and laude it over you. Or, you may believe that you will not match up to the famous person, changing your mood from one of joy, to one where you are exhibiting distress.

If you are positive and self-confident, none of these scenarios will be of any concern. You will be able to reason that this is a famous person who your partner may simply have a crush on, the possibility that they would leave you for that person is very low. You will then evaluate your positive attributes and how you contribute to the relationship. By the time you have completed this mind game and averted the scenario to one that has no basis to worry about, your partner would have already gone and come back to show you with excitement the autograph that they have received.

For every action, there is an equal reaction and this is applicable to your feelings. If you want to feel good, then you will do things that make you feel good. This simple analogy can help you build up your confidence easily. Jealous actions, anxiety attacks, and bursts of insecurity, these are emotions that do not feel good, and they should be avoided. Loving thoughts, planning for romance, trusting your partner, believing in them, these emotions make you feel good. Acting on these thoughts should bring more feel good situations into your personal space.

To feel more confident you have to let go of the payoff that you receive from insecurity. This may sound like a strange statement, especially when you know that insecurity is what we refer to as the uglier side of your personality. Sometimes, when you display your insecurity you get more love from your partner, they take time to allay your fears, and they could even go out of their way trying to show you how much they truly love you. For example, you are out for dinner and you notice for a split second, your partner admiring another person. As you pout and go silent, your partner begins to profess their love for you to reassure you that it is you they love not the other person. Then they are on their best behavior for the rest of the evening, making you feel good. They buy you flowers after dinner, and get you a gift on the way home to apologize. They keep asking if you are ok, and take responsibility for their split second glance. They feel so guilty and will do anything to make you smile again.

This can be highly addictive, and you may get stuck in a perpetual pity party, where you even begin to look for scenarios that will bring out your insecurity. When you are more confident and have a better self-image, then your partner will love you from a point of appreciation rather than as a result of guilt. You will still receive the love, and it is likely to be more genuine that it had been before.

So let's try an exercise: Find a calm, quiet place to sit, close your eyes and imagine that you arefully relaxed. Now, imagine a situation that would make you feel jealous, really jealous, and then deepen your breathing. Make your limbs relax and your heart rate slow, even as you imagine that terrible situation. A great way to do this is imagine that you're disinterested in that situation. The situation is separate from you, and does not say anything about you as a person. It does not say that you are less desirable or less attractive. It is simply you interpreting what you have seen your partner do. You know that your imagination can run away from you so you choose to let the entire situation go. Send it to the deepest recesses of your mind and completely ignore it. It is not bigger than you and it does not define you. This will help you take away the power from that situation, returning the power to you.

The final result will be your imagination being under control, and you will find that you actually have the ability to deal with the situation. This will instantly increase your self-confidence, and it is all in the mind. Remember that you are only, truly ever in control of yourself and your actions, and you cannot control another human being, nor should you try.

The more you're able to practice this deep breathing and calm detachment when you're in a situation that makes you feel jealous or anxious, the better you will feel about your partnership with your significant other. Where there were feelings of anxiety, there will now be feelings of trust. Where you were likely to rage at your partner, you are more likely to share your feelings in a calm way, so as to bring about mutually beneficial results. When you are more confident within your relationships, you cause an upset in the dynamics and your relationship has no choice but to mature into something fabulous.

Your expression of jealousy is more about self-love than focusing on the feelings of others. It is about how you are feeling in that moment rather than taking into consideration how others are feeling and that is why empathy is so important.

When you are confident in yourself, you are less likely to experience jealous feelings, and should they show up, you will easily be able to overcome them. So in order to overcome jealousy, you need to have a healthy dose of self-esteem. Learning how to overcome jealousy is not about making your partner change his or her behavior, it is about you being able to overcome your own behavior and learn that you are feeling a certain way because of yourself and not someone else.

Building your self-confidence is not something that occurs in an instant, although you can take actions that will show you immediate results. It takes time, and you should approach it one day at a time, and one thought at a time. To build your confidence and imagine yourself on top of your game, you can make some positive affirmations on a daily basis. Try the following:-

a) I am beautiful or handsome and worthy of love.

b) There is something about me that is pretty special.

c) The best part about being me is that I am completely unique.

d) I have so much to offer the world.

e) I can make a positive impact on my relationship.

f) I know that I can make today great.

There is power in speaking positivity into your life and your circumstances, and you have the ability to build yourself so that you can help your relationship.

To bring more positivity into your relationship, you need to behave in a more positive way. This entails you looking for the good in the relationship and in your partner. The true test for building trust and overcoming jealousy and anxiety will come about when you are facing a challenge in your relationship. It is very easy to lay blame, to accuse, to shout and to be right in a situation. It is much more difficult to look at the situation positively, and even in challenges bring out the best of yourself. If you are able to learn how to do this, then you can attract more positivity to yourself and your relationship.

5 Simple Things You Can Do To Help Adopt a Positive Attitude

Knowing that you need to adoptive a positive attitude is one thing. Reading about how you can try a few things to help boost your self-confidence is another. Sure, both of those things can help your relationship, but they are not the only things you can do to bring more positive and less negative into your relationship. Adopting a positive attitude towards life in general, not just your relationship is going to help greatly when it comes to getting over your own insecurities.

Therefore, with that being said here are 5 simple things you can do to adopt a positive attitude.

Know What You Want To Change

In order to adopt a positive attitude on life in general you need to know what needs to be changed about yourself. Identifying what needs to be changed isn't going to be easy, it is going to require some pretty deep soul searching. You have to really look at yourself and your personality traits to decide what ones need to be worked on and eventually changed.

Adopt a Role Model

One of the easiest ways to adopt the attitude that you want to have is to find somebody who has your ideal attitude. Now we are not saying to stalk this person and take over their life, but watch and learn from them. See how they react to specific situations and take your cues from them to help better yourself as a person.

Think About How This Will Alter your Life

To be successfully in embracing your new lifestyle change you need to understand just how it is going to alter your life. What you need to do is sit down and think about how you adopting a positive attitude will affect your current lifestyle. Ask yourself the obvious questions, such as if, the new attitude will make you and your partner happier or if it will generally make things more pleasant in your household. Once you have answered those questions, keep reminding of the positive results of this attitude change to help ensure your success.

Carefully Pick Who You Want Around

Your friends have a direct influence on your attitude. If you surround yourself with negative people, you are going to have no chance of adopting a positive attitude. This is honestly easier said than done because it sometimes involves drastic lifestyle changes. You need to carefully evaluate the people you currently surround yourself with and ask if they will be helpful in your journey to adopt a positive attitude. If they are going to be counterproductive to your goal, you will need to make the decision on whether or not to cut them out of your life. Bear in mind though that surrounding yourself with positive minded people makes it easier to make the change in yourself.

Believe in Yourself

This is something that we simply cannot stress enough. In order to change yourself, you have to believe in yourself. If you don't believe that you can change your attitude or anything else for that matter, you are never going to be successfully at doing it. Not believing in yourself is basically setting yourself up for failure. Not believing in yourself causes you to give up on yourself, which means you will never have the opportunity to succeed at changing your attitude.

Adopting a positive attitude will not only change your outlook on life, but it will also change the quality of your life. Having a positive attitude will improve your relationships with family, friends, and most importantly your partner. Now that you are no longer focusing on the negative things that might happen, you can focus on the good things that are bound to happen. Without the emphasis on the negative trust, insecurities, and other negative feelings in your relationship will quickly start to improve.

Chapter Ten:
Trust Issues in Long Distance Relationships

Thus far, the relationships that have been addressed are those where you and your partner are living together or have a close interaction. However, there are special relationships where trust can really be an issue, and those are long distance relationships.

A long distance relationship is one where you and your partner do not live near or with each other. Usually, you will be separated by at least a town or a state, and in extreme cases, this separation could be an entire country or continent. If you experience feelings of jealousy when you are with your partner and can keep track of what they are doing and their movements, imagine what it must be like if your partner is miles away from you, and you have no idea what they get up to on a daily basis.

In order to handle these trust issues, it is imperative to define what they are, and what could cause them. From that juncture, it becomes possible to overcome them. The most common issues that arise with trust in long term relationships are discussed in this chapter.

Physical Affairs

The biggest issue with trust arises with the suspicion that you partner may be having a physical affair. This fear becomes very strong when you are both separate by a large distance, and unable to see each other for months at a time. If you are both young, you may be concerned that your partner would seek someone to fulfill their sexual needs, and this would leave you feeling insecure and unable to function well.

When you suspect your partner of a physical affair, your imagination could run away with you, and you could find yourself plotting and planning all types of schemes to catch them at it. On the other hand, the suspicion alone might leave your devastated as you see the end of your relationship in sight.

The key to maintaining a long distance relationship lies in communication, and if you have open and honest communication with your partner, you should be able to keep it together until you see each other. When you distrust your partner, your communication may be strained, causing hurtful arguments even when you are so far away from each other.

Emotional Affairs

Another issue that deeply erodes trust is if your partner has an emotional affair. This type of affair is often more painful and difficult to deal with than a physical affair. This is because it goes to the core of the relationship, and creates questions about what the relationship is truly based on. You may feel that if your partner really loved you, why would they share the deepest part of themselves with someone else?

Trust can be irreparably damaged when one of the partners enters an emotional affair, because this requires an investment of time, as well as keeping secret contact with another person. When in a relationship, in order to maintain trust throughout, the partner needs to ensure that they are completely open in everything they do. There should be no secrets between them, especially when they are so far apart.

When secrets creep in, the relationship begins walking on a tight rope that can easily end in doom.

Facebook Dramatics

Facebook and other social networks have been at the root of many issues for people in long distance relationships, as these are open forums where people present information about themselves and their lives to the world at large. There are several factors that could cause trust issues for people who are in relationships, and on a social network. These include: -

- Hiding information – In a long distance relationship, you may demand a certain degree of openness from your partner. One of these demands may be that you share passwords to all your information – email, social networks and so on. That way, everything is open and clear. If your partner refuses to give you information, and instead, begins to increase their security features on the social network restricting your access to certain information, you may begin to distrust your partner. This sort of behavior leads you to question their motives.

- Un-friending your spouse – With the advent of technology, most communication in long distance relationships takes place online and through the telephone. On Facebook, once you are friends with your spouse, they instantly get access to some privileged information about you. In some cases, you may find that after an argument, your partner removes you from their friends list. This means you no longer have access, and they can do things privately, and behind your back.

  If you have been unfriended, it is likely that you will automatically begin to question the motives of your partner, and you will also begin to suspect them of some foul play. Trust will no longer reside in the relationship.

- Changing relationship status – Social networks are a way that you can speak to the world silently, without saying a word. You may develop trust issues if your partner changes their relationship status without letting you know. For example, a relationship may go from being In a Relationship to It's Complicated. This will raise your suspicions and create strain on a relationship that is already facing the odds when it comes to its survival and sustainability.

Secret Cell Phones

When in a long distance relationship, you are unable to monitor your partner as closely as you would if they were with you on a daily basis. Trust issues will arise if you discover that they have a cell phone that you knew nothing about. Even if this cell phone is used purely for work purposes, the issue is that they did not inform you of its existence.

When a partner has a secret cell phone, the presumption that they are being unfaithful comes to light. The trust can further be eroded if as a partner, you are unable to access the text messages, pictures or call lists to determine who is receiving communication from this phone.

The main challenge that people in long distance relationships face is being open, as this is the only way that you can rise above suspicion in all manner of incidences.

Hidden Emails

This is something that you will often stumble upon, and from that moment, you will become suspicious and distrustful of your partner. Picture your partner has come home for a visit with you, and they check their email using your computer or laptop. If they do not sign out, you may innocently find yourself in their email box. If you notice a special folder where there are emails from someone they are interacting with privately, you may become suspicious of their behavior.

The nature of the messages will also have an effect on how much you trust in that situation. If you are in a long distance relationship, there is a rule that you should live by to ensure that your relationship maintains a good level of trust and understanding. This rule is that if you know you are doing something that would upset or anger your partner if they knew about it, then you should not be doing it.

In a long term relationship, trust issues cropping up lead to the crippling of the relationship, as it is likely that one partner will completely shut down or find all sorts of ways to defend themselves – and these ways are often destructive. This is because the foundation of the relationship has been shaken, and the damage that occurs as a result is difficult to overcome. When you are in a healthy relationship you will have a loving connection. This type of connection will allow you to be open and vulnerable, no matter how far away you are from your partner.

The moment that you realize your trust has been violated, or if you are the one who violates the trust of the person that you love, you will experience a deep wound which will take a significant amount of time to recover.

Why do people break trust in long-distance relationships?

This is an important question to answer if you choose to overcome the issue of broken trust and move forward in your relationship with your partner. First, it is unlikely that your partner has a serious sexual addition problem or is unable to control compulsions. Although there are cases of this, it is not so for the majority of long distance relationships. Also, it is unlikely that your partner set out to hurt you.

Trust gets broken for other reasons, and usually, it will creep up on the situation rather than happen outright. It may come about because your partner is spending a considerable amount of time with a friend. Then the friendship goes out of control and before they realize what is happening, they are in the throes of an affair. Trust could also occur if the relationship is experiencing difficulty, and there are disagreements and frustration. When one partner feels as though the whole endeavor is hopeless, they may seek to find rest in the arms of another person. Usually this is something that happens spontaneously without much thought by the guilty party.

You need to learn how to deal with these trust issues because if you do not, you will carry them forward into every relationship that you get into in the future. Even though it may be a challenge to forgive and forget, it is worth a try as rebuilding the trust could actually lead to a stronger union in the long run.

What to do if you are the culprit

For the most part, this book addresses what it is like to be on the receiving end of broken trust or dealing with trust issues in a relationship, so what happens if you are actually the cause of the trust issues. First, you need to be sure that you are doing something wrong. If you have contemplated hiding an email, erasing your call log or putting a password on your phone to hide information, then you are already guilty of breaking trust. The key point to note here is the contemplation – not even the actually act with is obviously wrong.

The moment you violate your partners trust, especially when you are in a long distance can have detrimental effects and could mean the end of the relationship, whether you like it or not. Do not give in to the addictive nature that is at the root of infidelity. You need to give yourself a reality check, and realize that what you are doing may affect someone else for the rest of their life. It would be better to end the relationship, even if you have to do so prematurely, then to violate a person's trust.

You may be lucky in that you have spoken to your partner and they are willing to work through the issues with you, and get the relationship back on track. If this is the case, you will need to put in significant effort to regain their trust. It may mean that you invest more time in travelling back and forth so that you can spend time with them. You may need to be completely open with your partner, allowing them access to all your personal information, passwords and anything else that they demand for. Re-establishing trust will require significant sacrifice, but it is exactly what you need to do for the sake of your relationship.

Chapter Eleven:
Trust Issues and Mental Health

Someone may have broken your trust once in the past, and it hurt deeper than anything that you could ever imagine. Now you are carrying this pain with you in every relationship that you go into, and you feel as though it never goes away. Trust issues may not develop in your existing relationship as a result of the actions of your partner. In some cases, these issues will come up because of something that is happening with you, something that affects your mental health which you have to deal with.

This chapter shall touch on some of the mental health problems that may be contributing to your trust issues.

Depression

Depression is a terrible condition, and a person who is dealing with depression would find it challenging to trust other people, particularly because it is so difficult for them to trust themselves. When you are depressed, you tend to see negativity all around, particularly in those who are closest to you. Being in a relationship with someone depressed, means that you will be subjected to their paranoia and insecurity, and you need to be ready to take each day at a time.

Another trust issue you will find with people who are depressed is the likelihood that they will second guess themselves. Therefore, they will constantly be swaying in their minds when it comes to making a decision. This is because the relationship is so important to them that they get to a point where all they can think of is how to get it right.

To fully be able to handle your trust issues if dealing with depression, there is the need for intense therapy with a qualified psychologist. It cannot happen automatically, but it can improve considerably over time.

Anxiety Disorders

There are a whole range of anxiety disorders that could be contributing to your trust issues within a relationship. When you have an anxiety disorders, there will be actions or things that your partner will do which inadvertently cause you anxiety and trigger thoughts in your mind that make you question their motives.

One of the anxiety disorders that you may have is Paranoid Personality Disorder, which has the classic symptom of having a long-standing pattern of pervasive distrust and suspiciousness of others. This means that every time you are in a relationship, especially a romantic relationship, you find that you never really believe that your partner has the right motives, and you are constantly suspicious of them, and everything that they do.

The level of mistrust you have here should not be confused with the way you would react when dealing with a normal issue in your relationship. Here, your trust issue will come up before anything happens to warrant it, as you would be worried that everyone is out to exploit, harm and deceive you – without having any basis to support your thoughts. Your concerns would be extreme.

If you find that you are looking to consistently be self-sufficient, and you have a very strong sense of autonomy, you may be afflicted with this anxiety disorder. In addition, if your fear others are against you or persistently bear grudges, or find yourself constantly suspicious of the fidelity of your partner, even if there is no justification, this may be the problem that you need to resolve.

It is worth noting that these type of disorders are usually long standing and have with them enduring patterns of behavior. Therefore, you may not realize that you have something that is not right with you, until a competent psychologist is able to diagnose you. The older you get, the more extreme the symptoms.

Schizophrenia

Just like someone suffering from an anxiety disorder, if you have schizophrenia, you will also have an unhealthy dose of paranoia which will affect the level at which you trust people. This is the reason why this would be an issue in your relationship.

If you are the person who is to put trust into the actions of your partner, it means that you are agreeing to rely on their actions in the situations that you will face together in the future. In this scenario, as the person giving trust, you will allow the person whom you trust full control over their own actions, even if you may not be sure what the final result will be. You would believe that the person you trust will do what is expected of them. This is what you can expect from a normal relationship.

With a schizophrenic, this is far from what you will get. You would begin with a base where there is a base of mistrust, and this usually happens because of something that occurred in childhood that was beyond your control and your ability to deal with. Therefore, you approach all situations that deal with trust from a point of fear. This means that within a relationship, there are some issues that will become apparent.

The first of these would be your inability to get the relationship to the point where romance can develop. It is not so much that you believe your potential partner will cheat on you and betray you in that way, it is more that you expect them to hurt or disappoint you in some way and therefore you do not trust your feelings. You may also believe that all your friends are actually out to get you, and therefore, every time you are around them your thoughts race with suspicion about how they may hurt you. At the extreme, you may feel as though everyone is lying to you all the time, and this will lead you to be terrified of any physical intimacy with a partner.

If you have been diagnosed with schizophrenia, these are just a few of the issues that you may have about other people, and the only way to move forward is psychological treatment. If your partner has these types of issues due to this mental disorder, you should safely assume that it will be a long time before they get over them, and your relationship will be plagued with suspicion and insecurity.

Post-Traumatic Stress Disorder

This is a mental disorder that comes about following a traumatic even in your life, one where you were in danger and things were completely out of your control. After this type of experience, you will find it extremely challenging to trust other people again. This is not restricted to just your romantic partner, but it also controls how you interact with all other people that you come across.

What often happens is that you keep going back to the moment of your trauma, which is also the genesis of where your trust issues begun, and then you try to make sense of it. When you cannot, your emotions take over and these emotions include anger, fear and guilt. These are the basis within which trust is rooted.

The moment you need to interact with someone you love, you will find it a challenge to trust anything that they do, and therefore, you will find yourself avoiding them in many ways. This causes confusion for your partner, leading to arguments and setting up situations where you can justify your mistrust for them.

You could also find it challenging to get in touch with your emotions, though you will not be exempt from emotional outbursts when you suspect that your partner has betrayed your trust in some way – whether they have or not.

Social Disorders

If you have a social disorder, or are dealing with someone who has a social disorder, trust can be a great issue. There are many of these disorders which leave people crippled with fear, having panic and anxiety attacks and being unable to interact with people who are outside their immediate social circle.

If you happen to be within the social circle, you may have someone who believes that you will abandon them and does not trust in your ability to remain in the relationship. Therefore, they are always looking for avenues that they can create where you will let them down, and always emphasizing times when you did not live up to their expectations. Dealing with this type of mistrust can be challenging, not because you are not able to meet their expectations, but because you have someone waiting for you to make a mistake.

The best thing that you can do in this situation, or when dealing with a person who has this problem is to be open and honest with them in every instance. Keep to your promises as much as possible and ensure that you do not let the person down.

One element that appears to be prevalent in all these disorders is that there are possible delusions that accentuate the trust issues. This is where the person with the disorder sees things from an illogical perspective, or sees things that are not there at all. In addition to the accompanying mistrust, a person may also find themselves having hallucinations which further feed the paranoia and distrust.

The only way to move forward in this situation is to get medical treatment and back this up with some intensive therapy. Make sure that you do not get disheartened. Sometimes you can put a large amount of effort into building a relationship and you find that despite all that you have tried, your still cannot break down the barriers of mistrust. With mental disorders especially, healing happens in the long term and you may just have to accept that the relationship will remain the way it is.

Chapter Twelve:
Trust Issues and Financial Infidelity

There is the level of trust that you can expect to cultivate with your partner on a romantic level, and that deals with the feelings that are part of the foundation of your relationship. The infidelity that occurs with these feelings have been well addressed in this book, such that if you have a cheating partner or one who has considered being unfaithful, you are now armed with the right tools to handle the situation and overcome it if you wish to. Romantic infidelity is well discussed, and there is considerable support from various avenues to help you cope.

Financial infidelity on the other hand, is not well covered, which is surprising with its prevalence in relationships today. Financial infidelity is a term that refers to a situation where your partner cheats on you financially, by secretly spending money, or having credit cards that you do not know about. There could also be secret bank accounts or stashes of money hidden in places you have no access. On the negative spectrum, they could have accumulated substantial debt without your knowledge or your consent.

Financial infidelity can be devastating in so many ways, touching on the feelings that you had in the relationship and questioning the truth behind what has occurred in your relationship. To make it clearer, here is a scenario that you could consider.

You and your partner agree to combine your finances once you get married, so that it is easier for you to manage your home and also so that you increase your credit score. As you both cannot manage the account, you are fine with allowing your partner to do the main management, and simply give you money when you need it.

You sit together and draw up a plan. In your plan, you make room for catering to your daily and monthly expenses, investment as well as saving for the future. You have an idea of what you will be able to accumulate within the next ten years, and you are confident that you will be in a good financial place then to make a major purchase.

For several years, this system is working for you and then one day you happen to come across the financials file. Curious you look through it and then get the shock of your life. Between you and your partner, there is literally no money in the bank. There are no investments, and all the money appears to be in an account that you have no idea exists. The only money that is there is what you use from month to month.

When you raise this issue with your partner, you face anger for your interference, and that is when it really hits you that something has gone wrong. You are likely to feel as though you have lost years' worth of your hard earned cash, and are now in a financial position that had never been part of your master plan. You know that if you continue with this relationship and the way things are going, you will have no proper future.

The first thing that you need to deal with is your initial emotions, of anger, feeling betrayed and frustration. You have been cheated on, just not in the conventional way. The feelings are just as raw and intense, and you are going to need to deal with what this has done for your trust and your relationship.

Next, you need to find a way to deal with the issues and here are some pointers that will help you develop your trust again, and handle the betrayal you could be feeling.

- Discover where the problem begun – Before you entrusted your partner with your finances, you must have been sure that they were able to handle them. Married couples will share their nudity with more intensity that they share their finances. Therefore, trace back the steps. It might have innocently begun when your partner made a purchase, did not tell you, and got away with it. Or perhaps there was something that prompted your partner to open a bank account without your knowledge. In order to deal with the problem, you need to understand where it started and what caused it – only then can you begin to work on rebuilding trust.

- Pick up on little signs – It is likely that there were little signs along the way that pointed towards financial infidelity, but that you were too blind to see them for what they were. Little things like your partner changing the subject when you started talking about money, or items that had been purchased which you knew you could not afford. There could even have been a gift your partner got you (in an attempt to mask their guilt). By knowing how to read the signs, you protect yourself from further issues in the future sliding past you.

- Solve the problem first – Financial infidelity is not like romantic infidelity. You cannot leave it to fester while you consider how you should manage it. With financial infidelity you need to deal with the problem first, and then address the issues with your trust later. When left on its own, it could spiral out of control and become a problem that is bigger than you can handle.

- Start therapy – If you wish to overcome this issue in your relationship, you will need outside help in order to get to the point where you can trust your partner again.

Seek help from a therapy, and make sure that your partner is involved. Change the way that you approach money, and have them separate for a period of time, until your partner proves that they can be trusted again.

Financial infidelity can change the dynamic in your relationship, and the betrayal of trust will seep into every other area of your relationship and affect it, often negatively. Therefore, it is an issue that can ultimately bring the relationship to an end.

Dealing with this issue to ensure that trust comes back into the relationship requires the partners to be fully financially transparent, and this requires a plan of action to encourage this behavior. You may also need to create an agreement which you keep in writing for future purposes, so that you do not end up having a dispute over money. Rather, if one person does not keep up their end of the bargain, the consequences are clear.

Chapter Thirteen:
Reminding Yourself of Your Positive Traits

No matter how much your jealousy and insecurity has led to crazy behavior on your part, or maybe you have pushed your partner into a corner and are deeply ashamed of yourself, there is always going to be something redeeming about you. That is what probably keeps your partner hanging on to your relationship. There is no person who is all bad, everyone has some positive traits that they can expand on to improve their relationship.

Every once in a while, you need to bring to the forefront of your mind your positive traits and those of your partner. When you are in a difficult place within your relationship, the last thing you are thinking about is the positives, but that is where your mind needs to be. If you wish to remind yourself of your positive traits, there are some exercises you could try.

Think of people whom you have impacted in your life, and how it felt to help or assist them. Remember a time when someone said thank you to you for something thoughtful that you did. Picture a time when you made someone smile. These types of situations can point out your positive traits. There are many exercises that you can do to overcome your self-esteem issues, and let's face it, your jealousy stems from the feelings you have about yourself inside, not about the feelings you have for another person.

What is self-esteem?

Self-esteem stems from an early age where we barely even know our own names. It comes from the need for socialization, attention, love, safety, and belonging from our primary caregivers. When we're denied some of those needs, we develop problems with our self-esteem. Research has proven that even babies are aware of what is happening around them, and they begin to develop ideas and behavior from birth. In fact, self-esteem begins to develop when you are a child, when you have no control of what is happening to you.

For example, at a young age if you've been rejected by a friend, you might remember that you took this rejection personally. You possibly questioned yourself on how real your friendship was, and asked the question why without getting a proper answer. When something like this happens to you, it can have a profound effect on all your future friendships, you may even make the decision to never be rejected again. Your self-esteem can take a nose dive as you begin to wonder about what could be wrong with you; you also question why your friendship appears to be coming to an end. It is highly likely that you will believe there is something wrong with you rather than looking at there being something wrong within the situation. This in turn will affect how you behave from that point on.

In reality, a friend may have rejected you because of their own personal flaws and it had nothing to do with you, but you may not have had the right communication tools to really get to the root of the problem, so you made an assumption. Or they could have been going through their own transition in life, and found that you no longer fit into their plans. However, you may have turned to some internal problem you think you may have had, which this choice could stick with you for the rest of your life, especially if you don't figure it out and eradicate those thoughts.

You may notice that some people have been in similar situations and they do not have low self-esteem. So why is that? Well, there's such a thing called a shaming environment. It is where an individual who acts out believes they're not just behaving in a poor manner, but that they are actually a bad person. As an example, a child is sneaking cookies from the cookie jar and their parents continuously tell them they are bad rather than telling them their actions are bad. In that case, that child believes they are truly rotten to the core. Therefore, when they behave badly they justify their behavior by telling themselves that they are bad anyway, so there is no need for them to change.

If you were that child, and you grew up into an adult with these beliefs, then they will touch different aspects of your relationship. You are more likely to believe that you are bad when you make a mistake, rather than understand that you are not bad but that your behavior is wrong. These mistaken beliefs can lead to you treating your partner poorly because you feel continuous guilt for your behavior. To make up for the guilt, you may try too hard within your relationship, making your partner uncomfortable, while making yourself look desperate and confused. A strong relationship is not filled with a lack of trust or an overabundance of jealousy and anxiety. In order to develop a strong relationship, you must first address those issues. The same thing holds true for a fulfilling relationship, if you want one it cannot be based on guilt.

Children that grow up in that kind of environment tend to believe that the bad things that happen to them in life are deserved; that the good things are just flukes. If this mindset has become a reality, then it would be difficult to truly appreciate positivity in the relationship. One may always believe that their partner has an ulterior motive when they are being kind and building the relationship. So because they have guilt within them, they project mistrust on to their partners. They have internalized a negative event or string of negative events and it sticks with them. Others are able to see past this and the negative event rolls off their backs like water off a duck's feathers. When you can remind yourself of all your positive traits, you will be in a position to do the same thing.

As an adult, you can look at what happened to you as a child and realize that you were not responsible for your actions. You often did not know any better and were simply reacting to what you had been taught. If a child is able to believe that they are actually a good person that sometimes simply makes, then they're able to accept their flaws and try to make themselves a better person. People with low self-esteem have a distorted view of themselves and their actions. It is imperative to remember this when you are feeling jealous, anxious, or afraid. You have the control to improve the situation and as a result improve your relationship.

There are some steps that will help you eradicate that poor self-image. They are as follows:

1. Make a list of the positives about yourself and focus on those. You'll find that there are many more positives about who you are than there are negatives. As building your self-esteem takes time, you should try and add at least two items to this list on a daily basis.

2. Surround yourself with people who are uplifting and positive about whom you are as well as understanding about what you have gone through. This means that they need to have a certain degree of empathy and should not be judgmental. If you're constantly around negative people who take pleasure in pointing out your flaws, you will fail to see the positive in yourself and the world.

3. Do some charity work; if you are constantly helping out others or animals by putting their needs above your

own, you will find it harder and harder to feel bad about who you are; It is tough to feel guilty about spending time making someone else's life better.

4. Try meditation; sometimes reaching into that inner core and looking at yourself for who you are in a relaxing manner will help you understand that you are generally a good person. Meditation will reduce stress and make you feel less wound up when you are around your partner. When you are more relaxed, you can bring positivity into your circumstances much more easily.

5. Try exercising to relieve the tension in your everyday life. It will boost the hormones in your body that make you feel good, and this will help you feel better about yourself. In addition to the hormones, exercising will also help build your self-confidence as your body looks and feels better with time.

6. Seek out psychological help. If you feel that you're unable to do this on your own, there is no shame in seeking out help from a professional. Therapists and psychologists are well-equipped when it comes to dealing with self-esteem and jealousy issues. You can do it alone or you could bring in your partner for couples counseling so that you can better explain how you are feeling to them.

Once you have been able to build your self-image, you can easily focus on your positive traits. Focusing on your positive traits will lead you to a beautiful relationship – you will be able to conquer your feelings of jealousy, you will trust your partner and therefore experience decreased anxiety and as a person, you will bring in positivity into the union.

Adopting a positive attitude

The exercises we just mentioned are designed to help you be proactive in building up your self-esteem; they are things that can actually be accomplished each day. While these things can help boost your self-esteem, they are not the only thing that matters. If you really want to see a drastic improvement in your self-esteem you are going to need to work on your attitude. Only you have control over your attitude and your attitude is going to affect every aspect of your life, so you may as well adopt a positive one.

Turning your attitude from a negative one into a positive one is going to take some work. It is not something that is going to happen overnight, but you can start working on it as soon as possible. When changing your attitude you are going to need to work on how you react to the entire world around you, not just your current relationship.

If you are feeling a bit unsure, which is entirely natural, here are some things that you can do to begin the process today.

- Be aware of the progress that you have already made in your life and the progress that you continue to make each day. Acknowledge yourself; basically pat yourself on the back, for everything that you have accomplished. For what you haven't accomplished, don't worry or stress over it, you need to simply accept the fact that you haven't mastered it yet and then keep trying.

- Understand that there are going to be plenty of things in life that you can't control, learn what they are, as well as the things in life that you can control. By accepting the fact that you can't control everything you will save yourself from making repeated failed attempts at making the change. And the sooner you quit failing, the sooner you will begin to see an improvement in your attitude.

- Learn what you can from the mistakes that you make. Making mistakes is not always a bad thing, especially when you can learn something from the mistakes that you have made. Constantly dwelling on the mistakes that you have made causes you to live in the past and reinforces those negative feelings. To adopt a positive frame of mind you need to look past the mistakes and focus on improving your life and your relationship.

Like we mentioned before, building up your self-esteem and adopting a positive attitude is not something that is going to simply happen, especially not overnight. Making these changes is actually a life long journey; it is something that you are always going to have to work at. As with everything in life, some days are going to be easier than others. The worst thing that you can do is dwell on the negative days, you simply need to keep moving forward. And, remember to always give yourself credit when credit is due!

Boosting self-confidence

While it is important to work on improving your self-esteem, you must also work on boosting your self-confidence, which we kind of covered in the previous chapter. In this chapter, we are looking more closely at how self-confidence affects self-esteem. The more confident you feel about yourself, the less likely you are to be insecure in your current relationship. Many people assume self-confidence and self-esteem are the same thing, they even use the terms interchangeably. They are not the same thing, they are two totally different things, they just happen to be related to each other.

Self-confidence is how much you believe in yourself; how you believe that you can set goals and reach them. When you go about boosting your self-confidence you are enabling yourself to take better care of yourself, but you are also teaching yourself how to be happy and accept yourself for who you truly are. Boosting your self-confidence is vital if you are trying to improve your self-esteem because increased self-confidence provides a solid foundation for improving self-esteem.

Now self-confidence directly affects jealousy because of how you think of yourself. The lower your opinion of yourself, the more likely you are to be jealous of your partner. To ensure you have a healthy relationship, you are going to need to work on boosting your self-confidence. Luckily, there are few simple, but yet effective exercises you can start doing today.

Smile

This might seem a bit odd, but simply smiling more is a quick and effective way to increase your self-confidence. If you think about when you greet people with a smile, they are more likely to greet you with one back. And, the more people who smile at you, the better you feel about yourself. Plus, the more people you are smiling at, the more people you are helping give a self-confidence boost to.

Dress

How you dress honestly affects how you think about yourself. This might be hard to imagine, but take a minute to think about how you feel when wearing certain clothes. When you dress up and look nice, you tend to feel better about yourself. If you are laying around in frumpy clothes, like sweatpants and a holy shirt, you are not usually feeling your best. Everybody feels there best when they feel good about how they look, so pay attention to how you are dressing to ensure you always feel your best.

Mind

Many people underestimate just how powerful the mind is, but mind over matter is a very real thing. When you see or feel yourself thinking negative thoughts, you need to start redirecting your thoughts. When redirecting the thoughts, substitute the negative thoughts for positive ones. You will see immediate improvement about how you are feeling about yourself.

Exercise

It has been proven numerous times over that you always feel better about yourself after some good old fashioned exercise. Most likely because of all of the endorphins your body releases in response to the physical activity. However, exercise also helps you blow off steam, which reduces your stress level and helps improve your mind. If you are ever feeling down about yourself, go out for a quick jog around the block or even a power walk around the neighborhood can help.

In order to boost your self-confidence you are going to need to practice these exercises daily, how many you practice each day will depend on you, but the more you do the faster you will see an improvement. While practicing these various exercises, you must also see yourself making these improvements. The more you reinforce something, the more you are going to believe it. And, don't quit once you see an improvement, boosting self-confidence is a lot like improving self-esteem, it is a life long journey.

Chapter Fourteen:
Understand Trust to Resolve your Issues

Before you can begin to rebuild your trust, you need to understand trust. Think about it for a moment. Depending on the relationship that you are in, the way that you trust will be different. Therefore, you cannot describe trust as something that has the same standing in all relationships. This is because the type of trust that you give is based on specific contexts.

There are the contexts of the relationships, whereby you offer different levels of trust in a professional setting, personal, social and family settings. When your trust is betrayed in the work place, you are likely to get angry and annoyed, but you can usually recover from this relatively quickly. However, when your trust is betrayed in an intimate relationship, it cuts very deep, and you are likely to struggle with dealing with all that arises.

This chapter looks at the three levels of trust. Understanding them will help you overcome feelings of anxiety and insecurity that are often the basis for your trust issues. Although most of this book has been dealing with your romantic relationships, this chapter shall address the other relationships if your life that may be riddled with trust issues.

Deterrence-based Trust

This is the first level of trust that you can encounter and it is governed by rules. In all your relationships you will have some rules, and these rules may be written, spoken or even within you, but they are always in existence. From these rules, the relationship grows and therefore, they are fundamental.

The rules are there to protect you from being mistreated or taken advantage of from one person and they also serve as your personal compass, stopping you from doing the same to another person. If you think about society at large, these rules would be known as the laws that we live by, and in a company, these would be the policies and procedures.

Once you violate these rules, you have to face some consequences and punishments, and this is known by all.

Now, consider what these deterrence based trust rules would be in your relationship with your partner, as they are the basis of your trust. You may have an agreed rule that you will both be home with each other by 9 pm on a daily basis. You may also agree that anytime your family members come to visit, you will both be there to offer your support. Or that you have a date night every week on Thursday.

Trust issues start to creep in when you or your partner start to break these seemingly harmless agreements without a reason that can be easily justified. This is because there will be a dissatisfaction within the relationship, and this dissatisfaction shall continue to fester and grow the more that these agreements are broken. Then one morning you will wake up and realize that there are problems with trust within the relationship.

In this case, the issue may not have to do with anxiety, insecurity or jealousy, it is more that the foundation of the relationship has been shaken as one or both partners ceased to take this part of the relationship seriously.

Knowledge-based Trust

When you have been in a relationship for some time, you get to know the other person pretty well, and start to learn what you can and cannot expect from them. No person is perfect, so it is unlikely that you will appreciate every single one of their traits. However, you will have an adequate amount of experience to be able to tell how they would react to a situation, and how they would behave towards you.

This means that you are aware of what trustworthy behavior looks in your relationship, both from how you communicate and the way that your partner communicates. In this setting, your relationship can move on a day to day basis as you both find a comfort zone together.

When working in an office, this is the sort of relationships that you will expect to find. A boss or head of department will give out work for the day, and you as an employee will be able to do a certain amount of work each day.

In your personal relationships, your knowledge based trust can become an issue when your partner starts changing the way that they do things. Take for example something as simple as the morning routine. You are used to the following: Every morning when your partner wakes up, they go into the shower, brush their teeth and change into their clothes for the day. They then tell you good morning, go to the kitchen and prepare a cup of coffee for themselves and for you. Following a brief breakfast, they kiss you on the cheek and head to work, and you next see them in the evening.

Suddenly, this program changes. Your partner wakes up an hour earlier than usual, puts on their exercise gear and goes for a run. They come back and continue with their routine as usual. This goes on for a week (and has never happened before). Although you may not have any evidence of wrong doing on their part, they are doing something that is out of character which immediately arouses your suspicions. You begin to question why there is a sudden change in their routine, and the lack of trust finds its root from this point.

Identity-based Trust

This is the third level of trust and the most intimate one you will find in all types of relationships. At this level, your life is enmeshed with the other person that you are relating with, in such a way that they have an intense effect on your wellbeing and your core self. Here the other person can identify with you, by knowing your hopes and dreams, your fears and doubts, your fears and ambitions.

This is the sort of trust that develops over several years, and when you trust in this way, you have a heightened level of transparency and you allow yourself to be vulnerable with the other person. This is because from your experience the person has not taken advantage of you in any way. Here, the relationship has proven itself in various ways – there is the belief that one is loyal, that there is understanding and that you accept certain things about the person that you are in a relationship with.

This level of trust is not seen in relationships that you find at the work place. It requires a certain level of intimacy, and therefore is found within marriages, and relationships that you have with your children as well as immediate and extended family, and very close friends.

It has passed through the other two levels, and come out of each level successfully. There is openness and communicated, and almost no gossiping, backbiting or hurt from dashing ones hopes and dreams.

This causes the most devastation when the trust is broken, as usually, a person does not see it coming. When trust is broken in this type of relationship, it is a challenge for the one who has been hurt to find the ability to trust other people again with the same level of intensity.

Take for example a couple who have been married for 40 years, and are now in their sixties. They have set up a comfortable life for themselves, they are retired from their jobs, their children have left the nest and are living lives of their own, and they have the rest of their lives to live together happily. Then one of the partners develops a gambling problem and secretly eats through all the finances that they have saved up to enjoy in their retirement. One day they wake up, and they are destitute.

The partner who has been betrayed will not experience jealousy as if there had been an affair, instead there will be intense anger and a sense of betrayal, especially after all the years that trust has been built and developed. This type of issue may mean the demise of the relationship completely.

The only way that this situation can be resolved would be if the partner who caused all the damage finds a way to resolve the situation, and does so quickly, and apologetically. If this is not the approach used, the trust is gone forever.

Trust in romantic relationships especially has so many different dimensions. There is the trust at the core of the relationship which deals with being together, expressing love and respecting each other's feelings. That is what has been addressed the most in this book, as it is the most prevalent trust in relationships.

However, once this trust has developed, other things begin to fall into the umbrella of overall trust, and if these are abused or taken for granted, recovery of the situation is often more than difficult - it can be impossible.

Chapter Fifteen:
Rebuilding Trust Once It's Been Broken

All throughout this book we have talked about jealousy, anxiety, and insecurity and how the three of these things often lead to trust issues. As you are already aware trust is a big part of any kind of relationship, if you don't have trust you won't have a relationship for very long. As we have talked about in this book, sometimes the trust issues are not the fault of your partner, they are based on your previous relationships. However, sometimes it is the fault of your partner; they do or say something that shatters the trust you have gave them.

Once your trust in your partner has been shattered your relationship often starts to go downhill. You are literally second guessing everything that your partner says and does, and the reason for that is the lack of trust. Once the trust goes, so does the sense of security and safety you had in your relationship. Once trust is broken the feelings of love, respect, and friendship are often replaced by anger and fear. And, trust us a partner who doesn't trust their partner can do better research than the FBI.

Trust issues can stem from all sorts of scenarios, whether its lies or infidelity, the reason doesn't matter, just the end results do. Once that trust has been broken, it might seem like all hope is lost. I mean after all, how can you reasonably expect to trust that person again when you have never felt so violated in your life? Now even if your life currently right now is filled with nothing but arguments and everything seems hopeless, there are some things that can be done to help rebuild the trust that you two once had.

Step One: Come Clean

The first step that you will need to take when trying to rebuild the trust in your relationship is to come clean with what you have done. Nobody can move beyond the hurt and the anger, if you continually deny that it happened. You have to step up and take responsibility for what you did, which includes admitting what you have done. Taking responsibility doesn't necessarily mean including all of those minute details, sometimes sharing the details only causes more pain and anger, so be honest but don't over share.

Step Two: Be Aware of How you Act

You need to pay close attention to how you are acting. Being on the defensive or even acting casually about the problem at hand can have disastrous results. If you act like what you did doesn't really matter, your partner is not going to be very willing to work things out. You need to put forth a very sincere effort to show your partner that you do feel bad for what happened.

Step Three: Talk about It

After you have come clean about what you have done, you will want to find the time to talk to your partner about what made you do it. I don't recommend doing it right away, wait a few days for things to calm down a little bit. Talking about why you did it, how you might need help, as well as how you plan to fix things so it doesn't happen again is a great way to show your partner that you are serious about working things out, and just might convince them that you can be trusted again.

When you sit down to talk with your partner about everything that has happened it is important to do it correctly. When talking you want to sit so that you are facing each other, and as we learned from trust building exercises, as close as possible, to help reestablish that trust. Proceed to tell your partner the entire truth, do not go into hurtful details, but be honest about exactly how you feel. If you make things seem better than they are, you are not doing yourself or your relationship any favors. Honesty really is the key to rebuilding trust.

Step Four: Be Gentle

Communicating is vital to rebuilding trust, as long as it is done correctly. While you want to be perfectly honest and open with your partner, you don't want to be harsh. Coming right out and confessing might make you feel better, but it isn't how your partner deserves to be treated. Talking openly and honestly doesn't mean you have to forget about tact, you can still get your point across about how you are feeling while being tactful. And, no matter what happens or who confesses what, the worst thing either one of you can do is attack the other.

Step Five: Let your Partner Talk

Part of communicating freely involves letting your partner speak. This can be especially hard if your partner has recently hurt your feelings, but you won't be able to resolve anything if you don't listen to what they have to say. By listening to what they have to say, even if it's not something you necessarily want to hear, it is something that they need to do. It can also help you decide if it's worth trying to rebuild the trust, just don't make that harsh decision while you are still feeling angry.

When letting your partner talk that means they are going to also have questions. The worst thing you can do is avoid answering your partner's questions. No matter what question they have you need to respond to the questions, avoiding them make you seem guilty of something. And, remember, when answering their questions you need to remain honest, yet tactful. Belittling them or attacking them is only going to work against you.

Step Six: Be Transparent

In order to prove that you are doing everything that you can to be trusted again you are going to need to make yourself entirely transparent to your partner. Making yourself transparent to your partner includes giving them access to everything, emails, voicemail, etc. While this might sound easy, it really is not because you are simply giving up your privacy and that can make a person edgy. Being edgy often means you end up getting defensive with your partner, which can cause even more problems. Just remind yourself it's either your privacy or your relationship, only you can decide what one is more important.

In addition to being transparent with your partner, you also need to willingly share information. If you feel like you have to withhold information from your partner, you are setting yourself up for trust problems later on down the road. If it is something that you have to hide, either you shouldn't be doing it or you shouldn't be in the relationship. Being open and honest with your partner means they have less reason to doubt you when you tell them something.

Step Seven: Renewing the Vows

Most people think that in order to renew their vows they have to be married, but that is far from the truth. If you are simply in a relationship you and your partner need to sit down and talk about what you fist felt when you entered into the relationship. Talk about the values that both of you considered sacred. You need to have a serious discussion as to what you want and how you want things to be in the future. Each partner can write up their own vows and you can even perform a ceremony in front of your friends to help make it even more official.

The one thing that you need to remember when it comes to rebuilding the trust in your relationship is that it is not something that is going to happen overnight. Even though the trust was lost overnight, the actions that lead up to the loss of trust probably took place over an extended period of time. If you really want to rebuild your trust in your partner or you want to start believing in your partner again, you are going to need to put forth the effort required. You can't give up just because it's not easy.

Is it safe to trust again?

Once your trust has been broken, it can be very hard to trust that person ever again. We will be perfectly honest here, there is no way to guarantee that your partner won't break your trust again, but at the same time there isn't anything saying they will ever do anything to break your trust again either. This kind of puts you into a catch 22, and only you can decide if you are willing to take the chance and trust in them again.

Once you do decide to trust your partner again you are going to be overrun with various emotions. You are going to wonder if they are going to be betrayed by them again. Don't worry, these fears are 100% normal, but being aware of them is a good thing. These fears if left to fester in your head can be the downfall to your relationship, as they can get in the way of rebuilding trust and getting things back on track.

138

You end up being cautious because you are afraid to be hurt again, but being cautious can work against you and your goal of saving your relationship. Trying to move forward past the anxiety and insecurities can be very hard; it would be easier if you had a sure fire way of knowing that nothing like this would happen again in the future. If only there was some way to know for sure that your partner is telling the truth and they have changed.

There isn't a sure fire method out there that will tell you that your partner is trustworthy once again. But, there are several signs that you can watch out for in both you and your partner that can signal it is safe to trust again.

Communication is open not closed

Communication is important in any kind of relationship, but open communication is vital if you are trying to repair a relationship. Closed communication is not going to help solve anything, as both parties are keeping things bottled up inside. A sign that things are going better between you and your partner is when you are relaxed and listening to what each other has to say rather than not hearing each other. Pay attention when you are being open and try to incorporate those actions and words into each future conversation.

More Transparency

Now what you term transparency is going to depend on your own interpretation, but with a lack of trust it usually means full disclosure and access. When the partner that has betrayed the trust in the relationship is sincere about fixing things they often give their parent unlimited access to everything, including emails, voicemails, etc. They no longer have any secrets from their partner, but it has to be something they are willingly doing not being forced into. However, keep in mind that just because they don't give you full transparency doesn't mean they aren't trying. They could have a very valid reason as to why they are not giving you unlimited access to everything, so listen to what they have to say before judging them.

You are working together as a team

With this method you are going to have to pay attention or even reflect back on how things used to be, similar to the communication sign. When you are working together, you are listening to each other and learning from one another. When you work together you are not worried about proving somebody wrong or proving that your way is the best way, it's about appreciating each other and doing things together.

You notice improvement

Now the above mentioned signs are great at signaling improvement, actually realizing there has been improvement is sometimes a bit harder. In many cases one person sees it, while the other doesn't, usually because that person is still stuck on what happened before. If you are serious about fixing your relationship and rebuilding the trust that was once there you need to make sure you are looking at things that are happening in the moment. You don't want to ignore what happened in the past, but you also don't want to live in the past. Learn to recognize when you are getting stuck on what happened in the past and teach yourself to return to the present moment.

What you need to always keep in mind is that these signals mentioned above, are just a few of the things that you can watch for. There are numerous ways that your partner can show or prove to you that they are trustworthy again, you just have to be looking for the signs.

Chapter Sixteen:
Tips to help you Control your Trust Issues

There are many dimensions and levels that exist when it comes to trust and overcoming it, and you need to know how you can build trust in your relationship, and bring all the issues that come along with trust under control. By doing so, you are setting yourself up on a delightful path of long term happiness. Here are some quick tips that will help you deal with trust issues before they arise, and if you are in the throes of a trust issue, offer you some perspective.

- There is no such thing as a perfect relationship, so do not put that type of pressure on your relationship. There are instances where either you or your partner will mess up, and trust will be broken. Breaking of trust should not automatically mean the end of the relationship as you should take some time to try and resolve the problems first. Look at issues in communication, learn to handle problems from the root of the issue, and you will find that the intensity and occurrence of trust issues greatly reduces.

- Speak to your partner often, and allow yourself to be vulnerable. Many times, people choose to deal with trust issue by pretending that they are much stronger than they really are. If you want to create trust within your relationship, or to handle the trust issues that you already have, you need to let your partner see you when you are at your most vulnerable. That way, they will be aware of just how they made you feel, and if they were making an incident seem trivial, will likely change perspective.

- If your partner is the one who has the issues with trust, you need to work with them to overcome these issues. The first thing that you can do is be completely open with them in all your communication and everything that you do so that they see you have nothing to hide. Communicate well through conversation, and avoid snide remarks or abrupt answers. Then you can talk to your partner about the little things that you do each day so that they can feel more connected with you. Make sure that your partner knows the people that are in your life, and that they are able to connect and communicate with your circle of friends. By showing them that you care about their feelings and want to work on the trust, the issues can get quickly resolved.

- Appreciate what you have, and stop looking over your shoulder or around you to find out if the grass is greener. There are many trust issues that occur as a result of your misguided envy from looking at relationships in the media, or even comparing your situation with that of your close friends. Your relationship is unique and is yours, and you should not whine about it, instead you should work on it. The direction that it takes is in your hands, and if you need to work on your jealousy or that of your partner, do so, and then you will be able to move forward.

- Accept that you will occasionally make mistakes in your relationship, and make sure you are psychologically prepared to steer yourself in the right direction if need be. If you made the mistake of wrongly accusing your partner of infidelity, learn to apologies and improve your understanding of them and what they have to offer.

- Realize that the whole relationship does not rest on your shoulders, and you partner also needs to make a significant effort to making it work. If a trust issue arises, do not take it upon yourself to fix it in entirety. Ensure that you partner also takes some responsibility and works with you through the process of resolution. By working together on trust, you are likely to have a better relationship in the end.

- Trust is the foundation of your relationship. If you started off on the wrong footing, and have not trusted your partner completely from the get go, it will be quite challenging to develop trust as you go along. The same applies for your partner. If you were responsible for an indiscretion when you started your relationship, you should not be shocked if your partner does not trust you at certain times. Working on a relationship with either of these dynamics requires patience and effort for a great result.

- Secrets will be your undoing in a relationship, and therefore, if you want to avoid any issues around trust, you must ensure that there are no secrets between you and your partner. Everything should be out on the table, including your long term intentions for the relationship. If you are of the same mind-set, handling trust issues becomes easier to handle.

- As relationships develop, expectations arise, and changes need to occur. Usually, both partners are willing to change at the same pace ensuring that there is a balance in the relationship. However, there could be an instance where one party is more willing to change than another, and therefore, puts in more effort. This brings forth an issue in trust, where one partner may feel bitter and angry because of the effort that they have had to put into the relationship. They may not trust their partner's level of commitment. To build trust, there needs to be compromise and this in turn helps to take away any doubt that may exist about how much one is loved within the relationship. This takes away from the insecurity of no trust.

- No matter how much love that you have for your partner, if you are insecure in their love for you, trust will become very challenging to develop in your relationship. This is because you will constantly be wary of how much your partner loves you and is committed to your relationship.

- Do not be afraid to ask your partner for help when you are working out trust issues. Let them know what is frustrating you, and avoid snapping at them because you are hurt. In addition, avoid giving them the silent treatment so that they do not know how to communicate with you. If you leave the door of your heart ajar, you allow for them to come back in and resolve things with you.

- Get over the past. If you want your relationship to grow, you must leave the past behind you and move beyond the issue that is broken trust. Let your partner know of any triggers that take you back to the period where your trust was broken, and this makes it easier to avoid all of these triggers.

There are mental health conditions that can cause issues in trust to develop, and there are also mental health conditions that can occur as a result of a lack of trust in a relationship. The problems you could get include depression and frustration. You need to be careful with yourself and watch out for times when you feel as though you are losing control of your relationship and your partner. It is at this juncture that you should get some therapy and help, before your trust issues drive your partner away.

Conclusion

The next time you feel that you are becoming jealous of your partner or of anyone else, step back from the situation and evaluate it using the previously mentioned steps. Figure out why you are feeling the way you are based upon what has happened to you in the past, and remind yourself that you are in the present. Review whether you are looking at the situation through eyes of insecurity or realistically. Not every situation is going to be the same, and some may be more invigorating than others in a very bad way.

If you find that you are in a situation where you cannot control how you are feeling, you have every right to remove yourself from it. Exercise that right and keep your dignity intact as you do so. Politely excuse yourself from a party so that you can go home or take a moment outside to take a deep breath. Explain to your partner that you need a moment to yourself and accept that they are behaving the way they are because they want to. Do not try to control the situation with inappropriate actions, but rather take control of yourself and your feelings.

Learn coping habits so that you are able to better talk with your partner about how you feel, and if you are in a relationship with someone you suspect is a jealous lover, then confront them about it calmly. Do not allow their excited actions or anger provoke you into reacting in a negative manner. Instead, wait for them to calm down and try to discuss everything in an adult manner.

Remember that there is always help out therein some form or another, and you are not alone in your situation. There are many people who have battled with this monster, and they have won. So can you.

I hope this book was able to help you to find a great relationship for life.

The next step is to apply what you've learned in real life, as of today.

Would you be kind enough to leave a review for this book on Amazon? It would be very much obliged!

Emotional Intelligence

Develop and apply improved social skills and take control of relationships in your life

Table of Content

Chapter 1:
What Are Emotions?

What Exactly Is An Emotion?

The scientific answer to that would be that an emotional is a psychological state that has three different components: the subjective experience, a physical response, and a behavioral or expressive response.

There are many different ways psychologists have tried to come up with in order to explain emotions. In 1972, a psychologist by the name of Paul Eckman proposed there are six, basic human emotions that are universal. Those emotions include disgust, fear, anger, happiness, surprise and sadness. In 1999, he expanded that list to include excitement, embarrassment, shame, contempt, pride, amusement, and satisfaction.

In between Eckman's times, in the 1980's, Robert Plutchik suggested another classification system. This system was called the wheel of emotions. He suggested there are different emotions that can be combined with one another in order to create another emotion, just like an artist might mix together the primary colors to make another color. Plutchik proposes there are eight primary emotions: happiness, sadness, anger, fear, trust, disgust, surprise, and anticipation. When they are combined, they create another emotion. For example, when happiness and anticipation are combined, they may make excitement.

So what about the three different components of emotions? This may better help you understand your own.

Subjective Experience

Emotions are subjective even though all humans experience the basic, universal emotions. Regardless of our backgrounds or our cultures, we all experience the same basic emotions such as anger, sadness, or happiness. However, our experience of these emotions is actually unique. For example, not all anger is the same. There are subcategories of anger such as mild annoyance all the way up to blinding range.

We never seem to experience a pure form of each emotion, either. Mixed emotions over an even tor a situation your life is not uncommon. Those who are faced with a new job might feel both excited and nervous. Those who are having children or getting married might have anything from joy to anxiety, to all the emotions in between. They can happen at the same time or they may happen one after the other.

Physical Response

You've most likely felt your stomach lurch or twist when you're anxious or your heart palpate with fear. This is a physical response to your emotions. Many of these responses can include sweaty palms, a racing heart, and rapid breathing. These are all part of the sympathetic nervous system, which a branch of the autonomic nervous system. This part of your nervous system controls the body's fight or flight response, and when faced with a threat, these responses prepare your body to flee or face a threat.

Early studies of the physical forms of emotion focused on autonomic response, recent research has targeted the brain's role in your emotions. Brain scans show that the amygdala, a part of your limbic system, has a role in your emotions, especially fear. This is a tiny, almond shaped component of the brain that has been linked to hunger and thirst, as well as emotion and memory.

Behavioral Response

This final component is most likely the one you are most familiar with, the expression of emotions. We spend a lot of time interpreting emotional expressions of those around us, and our ability to accurately understand the expressions of their emotions is what gives us emotional intelligence. These expressions play a large role in our body language. Expressions such as smiling or frowning are universal across the globe.

Our culture also plays a large role in how we express emotions. For example, in Japan, those who are in the presence of an authority figure mask their fear or disgust. They almost seem to shut-down.

Emotions vs. Moods

Did you know that your emotions and moods are actually different? An emotion is something that is short-lived and intense, and they're likely to have a definite and identifiable cause. For example, you may feel angry after an argument with a friend or lover.

A mood is a milder version of an emotion that is longer-lasting. It's usually hard to determine the specific cause of a mood. For example, you may feel sad or lonely for several days without a real reason to feel that way.

Emotions Can Motivate Us to Take Action

Let's say you're facing an exam in the morning that you know is going to be very difficult. What motivates you to study in order to pass that exam? The fear or anxiety you're feeling of failing that important exam. You experienced motivation due to your emotions.

People usually take action in order to experience a positive emotion and minimize their risk of feeling a negative emotion. For example, a person might try to find social activities or hobbies that leave them feel content, happy, and excited. They may also avoid a situation that could lead to sadness, boredom, or anxiety.

Emotions Help Us Survive, Thrive, and Avoid Danger

Darwin believed that emotions were adaptations we developed in order to survive and reproduce. Anger made us confront the source of our irritation, and fear made us flee the threat. Love helped us find mates and seek out reproductions. Emotions are an adaptive role in our lives that motivate us to take action that will maximize chances for success.

Emotions Can Help Us Make Decisions

We may think that our decisions are guided purely by logic and rationality, but our emotions always play a role in our good decision making process. In fact, research on those who have damage to their emotional intelligence shows that they make poor decisions, while those who have good emotional intelligence have excellent decision making skills.

Emotions Allow Other People to Understand Us

Interaction with others is something that happens on a daily basis to us, and it's important that we give them emotional cues to help them understand what we're feeling. These cues can include body language like facial expressions, or stating how we're feeling directly. When we tell someone we're feeling sad, happy, frightened, or excited, we're giving them imperative information that allow them to take action.

Emotions Allow Us to Understand Others

The emotional expression of others around us provides us with a wealth of social information. Communicating socially is an imperative part of our daily lives and relationships, ad when we can interpret and intact with those emotions of others, we're able to build stronger relationships. It allows us to respond in a deeper, more meaningful way that helps us strengthen the bonds with one another.

Darwin was one of the earliest researchers who scientifically studied emotions. He suggested that they are displayed in order for our survival and safety. For example, coming across a hissing or spitting animal tells you the animal is angry and upset. You are more likely to stay away and survive by not getting injured. In addition, we need to be aware of each other's emotions in order to stay out of stressful, dangerous situations and learn how to defuse them successfully.

Chapter 2:
What Is Emotional Intelligence?

What Is Emotional Intelligence?

Your emotional intelligence is your capability to identify, use, understand, and manage your emotions on a positive way to relieve stress, communicate in an effective manner, empathize with those around you, overcome daily challenges, and defuse conflicts. It can impact many different aspects of your life, such as your behavior and how you interact with those around you.

If you have a high emotional intelligence, then you're able to see your emotional state, as well as the emotional state of those around you. You can engage with the people around you and draw them to you rather than push them away. You can use your understanding of their emotions in order to relate to them better, and form healthier relationships. You can also use it to achieve more success at work and lead a more fulfilling life.

Your emotional intelligence has three different attributes. These attributes include:

- Self-awareness: Your ability to see your own emotions and how they're affecting your thoughts, behavior, and actions. It's also your ability to recognize your strengths and weaknesses, and your level of self-confidence.

- Self-manage: This is your ability to control your spontaneous feelings and actions, as well as manage your emotions in a healthy manner. Those who can self-manage can take initiative, complete commitments, and adapt to their circumstances.

- Social awareness: This is your ability to understand the emotions, concerns, and needs of those around you by picking up on their emotional cues, your ability to feel comfortable in a social setting, and how to recognize the dynamics of a group or organization.

Characteristics of Emotional Intelligence

According to Daniel Goleman, there are actually five elements to emotional intelligence. You'll recognize some of these from the previous chapter, but we're going to expand upon them.

Self-awareness

You already know that self-awareness is your ability to understand your own emotions, and that you don't allow your emotions to rule over you. Those who are self-aware are confident individuals because they're able to allow their intuition to take control rather than letting their emotions take control.

Those who have self-awareness first must be able to take an honest look at themselves and know their strengths and weaknesses. They work on those areas in order to perform better.

Most psychologists believe this is the most important part of emotional intelligence.

Self-regulation

When you're able to control your emotions and impulses, you have self-regulation. Those who are able to self-regulate do not allow themselves to become jealous or angry, and they do not ever make carless, impulsive decisions. They are able to think before they act. Some characteristics of this ability to self-regulate include comfort with change, thoughtfulness, integrity, and the ability to say no to others.

Motivation

Motivation plays a key role in having a high degree of emotional intelligence. Those who are motivated are able to defer immediate results for long-term success. They're productive, enjoy a challenge, and are effect in whatever they do.

Empathy

This is considered the second most important part of emotional intelligence. Empathy is your ability to identify with others and understand their needs, wants and viewpoints. Those who have empathy are excellent at recognizing other's feelings, even when they are not obvious. Empathetic people are great at managing relationships, relating to others, and listening. They do not judge quickly and avoid stereotyping others, and they live their lives in an honest and open way.

Social Skills

It's easy to talk with and like people who have excellent social skills, which is another sign of high emotional intelligence. Those who have strong social skills are team players and focus on helping others before they focus on their own success. They manage disputes, communicate effectively, and are masters at relationships.

Why Is Emotional Intelligence So Important?

Emotional intelligence is very important for everyone. We know that those who are the smartest are not always the most successful or the most fulfilled in their lives. We all know someone who is academically brilliant but they're not socially graceful and they're unsuccessful in their work or their personal relationships due to their ineptness. Our intellectual intelligence is not enough for us to be successful and happy in life. Your intellectual intelligence or IQ can get you into college, but your emotional intelligence is what will help you manage your emotions and the stress when you're facing final exams.

So what areas of your life does emotional intelligence affect?

- Work: Your emotional intelligence affects your work life significantly. If you have a high emotional intelligence, you can navigate the social complexities of your workplace and lead or motivate others. You can excel in your career. When it comes to gauging job candidates, companies view emotional intelligence as more important than technical ability and require emotional intelligence testing before they hire candidates.

- Physical Health: Chronic stress is a serious condition for those who are unable to manage their emotions. It leads to some serious health complications such as raised blood pressure, a suppressed immune system, an increased risk of heart attack and stroke, infertility, and a speed up of the aging process. Your first step is going to be learning how to relieve stress if you have a low emotional intelligence, but we'll get to that in later chapters.

- Mental Health: Chronic stress is also very detrimental to your mental health, and makes you vulnerable to illnesses such as anxiety and depression. If you're unable to manage or understand emotions, then you won't be able to manage mood swings. This can lead to the inability to form or manage strong relationships, and this leads to you feeling lonely and isolated.

- Relationships: If you have a stronger emotional intelligence level, then you are able to forge strong relationships with those around you because you can control your emotions and gauge the emotions of those you're speaking with or just being with. This can help you both in your personal and work life.

Chapter 3:
Emotional and Mental Intelligence

What Is Mental Health Or Emotional Health?

Your emotional and mental health refers to your psychological well-being. It includes the quality of your relationships, how you feel about yourself, and your ability to manage your emotions and deal with difficulties in a calm manner.

A good mental health is not just about the absence of mental health problems. It's about being free from anxiety, depression, and other psychological issues. Mental and emotional health refer to positive characteristics. Remember that feeling bad is not the same as feeling good, and while some people may not have negative feelings, they need to do things that make them feel positive in order to feel mental and emotional health.

Those who are mentally and emotionally healthy have:

- A zest for life, laughing and fun.

- A sense of contentment.

- The ability to handle stress and brush past adversity.

- A sense of meaning in their relationships and activities.

- The flexibility to adapt to change and learn new things.

- A balance between their work life, play life, rest, activity, etc.

- The ability to create and maintain a fulfilling relationship with themselves and others.

- High self-esteem and self-confidence.

When you harbor these characteristics of mental and emotional health and stability, you're able to participate in life to the fullest by being productive and having meaningful activities and relationships. When you have these characteristics, you're able to weather life's challenges and stressful moments.

The Role of Resilience in Mental and Emotional Health

When you are emotionally and mentally healthy, it doesn't mean that you don't go through some bad times in your life or experience some emotional problems. Everyone goes through loss, disappointments, and change. They're all normal parts of life that cause anxiety, sadness, and stress.

However, those who have a healthy emotional outlook are able to deal with those moments and bounce back from the trauma, adversity, and stress. This is known as resilience.

People who have tools for coping with those difficult situations and maintain a positive outlook are able to stay focused, creative, and flexible during the bad times, as well as the good.

As aforementioned, one of the key components to having a healthy emotional outlook is being able to balance your stress and your emotions. Your ability to recognize and express your emotions appropriately will help you avoid becoming tuck in anxiety, depression and other negative mood states. You also have to have a strong support network. Being able to trust people and having them around you turns you toward encouragement, which boosts your resilience during those tough times.

Physical Health Is Connected To Mental and Emotional Health

Your body's needs should be of your first concern when it comes to your emotional and mental health. Your mind and your body are linked in a powerful way, and when you improve your physical well-being, you will experience a greater mental and emotional well-being. Exercise strengthens your heart and lungs, and it also releases endorphins that energize and lift your mood.

The activities you perform on a daily basis affect the way you feel emotionally and physically.

Here are some ways to improve your physical health:

- Get rest. When you get enough sleep, seven to eight hours every night, you're able to function with a more clear-headed mind. Without enough sleep, you can develop a short fuse which leads to outbursts.

- Learn about nutrition and practice it. First, do some research on what you should be eating and things you might want to avoid, like excess sugar and processed foods. Then, keep a diary of what you eat on a daily basis and how you feel after you eat those foods for a week. You'll start to see patterns as to what foods might aggravate you and what foods help you stay focused and alert.

- Exercise in order to relieve stress. You don't have to go to a gym in order to boost your endorphins and make yourself mentally happier and healthier. Just take the stairs instead of the elevator or take a walk at lunch for fifteen minutes. Instead of taking the first bus stop, walk to the second one. There are many ways you can add exercise into your daily routine.

- Get some sunlight. You should have ten to fifteen minutes of direct sunlight every day. You can do this while gardening, exercising, or even socializing.

- Limit your alcohol and drug consumption. This includes cigarettes. All of these are stimulants that make you feel good for the short term, but they have some long-term negative side effects for not only your body, but your emotional and mental health, too.

Improve Mental and Emotional Health by Taking Care of Yourself

If you want to maintain and strengthen your emotional and mental health, you have to pay attention to your needs and feelings first. Do not allow stress and negative emotions to build up, but instead try to maintain a balance between your daily responsibilities and the things that make you happy. If you take care of your needs first, you'll be able to deal with challenges when they arise in a much more positive manner.

Taking care of you includes some of the following:

- Do things that positively impact others. When you're being useful to others and being valued for what you're doing, you're building your self-esteem and self-confidence.

- Practice self-discipline. When you practice self-control, this leads to a sense of hopefulness and help you overcome despair.

- Learn to discover something new. Think of discovering something new as intellectual candy. Join a book club, take an adult educational class, learn a new language, visit a museum, or travel somewhere new, even if it's just a town in the same county you live in.

- Enjoy the beauty of art or nature. Studies have shown that those who take the time to smell the roses and view nature are able to lower their blood pressure and reduce their stress. Just sitting on the beach can be a great way to relax your nerves.

- Manage your stress. Stress is our enemy. It used to be necessary for short bursts of time to survive in the wild, but we're not chronically stressed, which can lead to heart disease and many other nasty illnesses. Try taking some stress management classes or utilizing some of the stress relieving tips found later in this book.

- Limit unhealthy habits such as worrying. Stop becoming absorbed in repetitive mental habits, such as negative thoughts about yourself and the world. These drain your energy, suck up your time, and trigger feelings of fear, anxiety, and depression.

- Appeal to your senses. Be sure to remain calm and energized by appealing to your five senses. Listen to music, put some flower on your desk, massages your hands, or drink a warm cup of tea or hot cocoa. Indulge yourself!

- Engage in creative, meaningful work. When you do something that challenges your creativity and makes you feel productive, you boost your confidence and esteem levels. Try something such as writing, gardening, drawing, building something or playing an instrument.

- Get a pet. You're right, they're a big responsibility, but caring for one makes you feel loved and needed. Pets give you unconditional love and they don't care about who you fought with that day or whether or not you forgot the milk. They're always waiting for you when you get home and they're never in a bad mood.

- Make leisure time a priority. Play-time for adults is just as much a necessity as it is for children. We need to engage in leisure time in order to unwind from a hard day at work.

- Make some time for appreciation and contemplation. Think about everything you're grateful for and take some time to meditate, enjoy the sunset, or take a moment to pay attention to what's positive, good and beautiful throughout your day.

Remember that everyone is different and not everything that is good and beneficial to you will be the same for others. Some feel better when they're relaxing while others need stimulation and excitement in order to feel better. Just find the activities in your life that make you feel boosted and energized.

Risk Factors for Mental and Emotional Problems

Mental and emotional health is shaped by experiences. Your early childhood experiences and memories are very significant. Genetic and biological factors may also play a role, but these are usually shaped and changed by experiences, too.

There are some risk factors that are able to compromise your mental and emotional health. These factors include:

- A poor connection or attachment with a primary caretaker in early life. If you felt abused, lonely, isolated, unsafe, or confused as an infant or as a young child, you are at a higher risk for mental and emotional complications.

- Traumas or serious loss, especially earl in life. These might include experiencing a war, hospitalization, or even losing a loved one such as a parent or grandparent.

- Learned helplessness. Sometimes people experience negative experiences that lead to a belief that they're helpless and do not have any control over situations in their life.

- Illness. Chronic or disabling illness that isolates children from others can cause emotional and mental distress.

- Medication side-effects. Those who are older who are taking many medications are more at risk for experiencing side-effects, which can lead to emotional distress.

- Substance abuse. Abusing alcohol and drugs can cause mental, physical, and emotional problems.

Whether you've had internal or external factors that shaped your mental and emotional health, it's not too late to make the necessary changes in order to improve your psychological well-being. These risk factors can be counteracted with protective factors such as a healthy lifestyle, strong relationships, and coping strategies that help you manage stress and your negative emotions.

When to Seek Professional Help for Emotional Problems

Sometimes, no matter how hard we try to do it alone, we need a professional to help us with our mental and emotional health. There's no shame in asking for help, and taking that leap will help you improve greatly.

Some red flag emotions and behaviors include:

- Insomnia

- Feeling helpless and hopeless consistently.

- Having problems concentrating at work and at home.

- Using food, nicotine, drugs, or alcohol in order to cope with your emotions.

- Self-destructive or negative thoughts or fears that you can't seem to control.

- Thoughts of suicide or death.

If you have any of these red flags, then it's best that you seek immediate treatment from a professional.

Chapter 4:
Developing Emotional Intelligence

Do you have emotional intelligence? The truth is that everyone has some level of what is referred to as emotional intelligence – some people just have more of it than others. If you are lacking emotional intelligence, luckily you can learn to develop more of it and use it in your everyday life. But first, how do you know whether you have a lot of emotional intelligence, or only a little? In order to answer this, you will first have to understand what emotional intelligence is.

Emotional intelligence is all about being able to know what people around you are feeling – what their emotions are. People with high emotional intelligence can easily tell what people they are associating with are feeling, and can then use it to benefit both themselves and others. If you understand what others are feeling, you will know how to treat them, talk to them, successfully work with them, and so much more.

You are probably wondering how you can develop your emotional intelligence. Well, you need to try to be more aware of your surroundings. Next time you are around others, try to take in all the little things about them that can signify what they are feeling. Are you someone who is generally caught up in a million things at once? Are you often stressed, worried, and frazzled? If this sounds like you, then you might be having trouble developing emotional intelligence because you don't take the time to focus on what is going on around you - you are always caught up in other things.

To develop your emotional intelligence, try practicing mindfulness. Mindfulness is just focusing on the present – instead of what might happen in the future or what has happened in the past. It sounds so simple, doesn't it? However, the truth is that with all the distractions of life, putting it into practice can be another story entirely.

You will have to work at it – so don't be discouraged if at first you fail. Practice again and again, and you will find yourself getting better at truly living in the present moment. In order to practice mindfulness, it is essential to be calm. So, you may need to do some breathing exercises to get rid of any stress or anxiety. This will hopefully allow you to be calm enough to focus on only what is going on around you, instead of worrying needlessly about other things.

How will this new skill called mindfulness help you develop your emotional intelligence? Well, if you practice mindfulness when you are around others, you will be able to easily pick up on their emotions. You will be focused on the present, which make you a lot less likely to miss a sudden change in, for example, someone's face or voice. It is the little signs like these that can tell you how someone is feeling – and in order to notice them, you need to be completely focused on what is going on around you.

Hopefully these tips will help you develop more emotional intelligence in no time. To quickly summarize the key points of this chapter, be sure to remember how important it is to get rid of stress so you can focus on the present. This will increase your emotional intelligence greatly. But, now that you have greater emotional intelligence, you need to learn how to apply it in everyday life. If correctly applied, emotional intelligence can be extremely helpful. Keep reading to learn how to apply emotional intelligence in your life. Emotional intelligence can help you develop and sustain the relationships you have always wanted. With emotional intelligence, you will have more control over the relationships in your life. If you want to improve a relationship that you feel needs work, you will be able to. If you want to mend a friendship, it won't be as hard. Your family and work life will greatly benefit from your new skill – so don't wait any longer! The next chapter of this book will help you on your journey to improving the relationships in your life.

Chapter 5:
Applying Emotional Intelligence

In the last chapter you learned how to develop more emotional intelligence. Hopefully you are starting to apply these tips and ideas in your own life – but you may be having some trouble with that. Maybe you don't know exactly how to apply emotional intelligence to you everyday life. Well, applying emotional intelligence is just about learning how to use it to help you develop and grow relationships to their full potential.

To apply your newly developed emotional intelligence, you will need to first think about the situations that it will be useful in. So, think about this: are there any relationships in your life that you need to improve and work on? Is there any area in your life where you are having trouble with relationships: whether this may be personal or professional? The first step to developing these relationships is recognizing what situations require emotional intelligence, and what situations require you to use more emotional intelligence than others.

So, think about the situations that you encounter in day to day life which could be made easier if you were to simply apply some emotional intelligence. What interactions with others are difficult? What relationships are faltering or even falling apart? Now you know where to apply emotional intelligence. The next step is to know how to apply it to the specific situation.

In order to apply emotional intelligence, you will need to recognize these situations and then remember to take others' emotions into consideration when you are in these specific situations. Some situations will call for more emotional intelligence than others. These are situations where you are really struggling – but with emotional intelligence, you will find a way to work out these problems in no time at all.

For example, if you are always arguing with someone, and can sense your relationship with them is gradually deteriorating, this is a situation where emotional intelligence can be a great help. With emotional intelligence, you can take the steps to gradually mend your relationship and become a happier, healthier person as a result.

First, take a step back from the situation and think about how you can apply emotional intelligence for the benefit of the relationship. Then, try to really focus on understanding what the other person is feeling and going through. Try as hard as you can to read their subtle voice tones, body language, reactions, and anything else, so you can figure out what emotions they are experiencing.

So, what do you do once you have some sort of idea of their emotions? The next step is to use this new knowledge to treat them accordingly, talk to them in a way that is best considering what their emotion is at the moment, and just interact with them in a way that takes their emotions into consideration. So, for example, if they seem to be having a very hard day, you would talk to them in a tone that might make them feel better. Of course, this is only one example – you will have to figure out how to apply your emotional intelligence to the specific situations that have occurred or will occur in your everyday life.

My hope is that now that you know more about how to apply emotional intelligence, you will find ways to strengthen the relationships in your life and build new ones that you never would have been able to build before. Between the information from this chapter and the information included in the last, you already know a lot about emotional intelligence and how you can use it in terms of relationships.

In the next two chapters, we will get more specific and delve into two particular categories of relationships. This will help you to learn about situations on a more specific and case by case level – but of course, in the end you will still have to tailor all of this knowledge to fit your own unique circumstances.

The next chapter will focus on how you can use emotional intelligence in your personal relationships. You will learn how you can start helping these relationships right now by simply applying the emotional intelligence that you have developed. In this chapter, the focus will be specifically on family relationships. This will include relationships with both members of your immediate family and your extended family.

Chapter 6:
Raising Emotional Intelligence

How to Raise Your Emotional Intelligence

So you know that you have a low emotional intelligence, but how do you boost it?

The information around use comes to the brain from our senses, and when that information becomes overwhelming or stressful to use, instinct takes over and we act with fight, flight or freeze. In order to have access to a wider range of choices and the ability to make good decisions, we have to be able to bring our emotions into balance when we need to.

Our memories are strongly linked to our emotions, and when we learn to stay connected to the emotional part of our brain at the same time we're connected to the rational part, we're expanding our range of choices and factoring emotional memory into our decision-making processes. This helps you stop continually repeating earlier mistakes.

In order to improve emotional intelligence and decision-making abilities, you have to first understand your emotions. Then you have to manage them. This can be accomplished through practicing and maintaining key skills that help you control and manage the overwhelming stress of everyday life, and helps you become an effective communicator.

You can develop emotional intelligence using a few key skills.

Emotional intelligence can be built by lowering stress levels, remaining focused, and becoming and staying connected to those around you and yourself. You can do this through a few key skills. The first two are imperative for controlling and managing your stress and the last three will improve your communication with others. Each skill it built upon the last skill, so you must start with the first one and work your way down.

These skills include:

- Reducing stress in stressful situations.

- Recognizing emotions and keeping them from overwhelming you.

- Connecting emotionally with those around you with nonverbal communication.

- Using humor in order to stay connected, even in a challenging situation.

- Resolving conflict through positivity and confidence.

You can learn these key skills at any time, but there is a different between learning about emotional intelligence and applying it to your life. Knowing that you ought to do something doesn't mean you will, and it's especially difficult when you've become overwhelmed by stress.

In order to permanently change your behavior and stand up under pressure, you have to learn how to overcome the stress in the moment and the stress in your relationships by knowing when your partner is feeling stressed. This means that you can't just read about it in order to master it. You have to practice the everyday skills in your life.

So here are the steps to reducing your emotional stress and building your emotional intelligence.

Reduce Stress in the Moment

High levels of stress can really overwhelm your mind and body, and they get in the way of your ability to accurately understand a situation. You lose the ability to hear what others are saying, what they're feeling or might need, and how to communicate in a clear and concise manner.

When you learn how to calm yourself down and relieve that stress in a stressful moment, you learn how to stay balanced, focused, and in control no matter what challenge you may be facing.

Try the following three steps in order to rid yourself of stress in the moment:

1. Realize that you're stressed. I know it may seem silly, but sometimes we don't understand that we're actually stressed out. We don't know the warning signs that stress is overwhelming us, like a quickened heart rate, increased breathing, muscles tensing, stomach being tight or sore, hands clenching, or even tears of frustration. Being aware of your physical responses allows you to regulate the tension as it is occurring.

2. Identify your stress response. Each person reacts in a different way to stress, and if you tend to become angry or agitated under stress, you're going to need different techniques than someone who becomes withdrawn or depressed. Those who become angry need quieting activities while those who become withdrawn or depressed need stimulating activities. If you freeze up, you may need to speed up in some ways and slow down in others.

3. Discover the techniques that work best for you. The best way you can reduce stress in the moment and rapidly is by engaging one of your senses such as sight, smell, sound, taste, or touch. People respond differently to sensory input, so you have to find the ones that are soothing or energizing to you. If you're a visual person, you might try surrounding yourself with uplifting photos, or if you respond to sound, you might want to try a wind chime to reduce stress levels. Each person is different, so you have to explore your needs emotionally in order to figure out what will work best for you.

Develop Emotional Awareness

When you are able to connect to your emotions and have a moment-to-moment awareness of what those emotions are and how they're affecting your thoughts and actions, you are able to understand yourself and remain calm and focused in a tense situation with someone else.

There are many of us who are disconnected from our emotions, especially the core ones such as sadness, anger, joy, and fear. This can be a result of a negative childhood event that taught to us keep our emotions hidden and to shut them off. We may be able to deny, distort, and numb our feelings, but we cannot seem to eliminate them, so we must know how to deal with them. They're still present in our everyday lives and without emotional awareness, we cannot understand our motivations and needs, or communicate them with others. We're at a far greater risk of becoming overwhelmed in a situation that may appear threatening.

In order to understand your emotions, you must first identify with kind of relationship you have with them.

- Do you have feelings that flow, coming across one emotion to the next as your experiences change throughout the day?

- Are your emotions coupled with physical sensations that you experience in areas such as your chest or stomach?

- Do you experience discrete emotions and feelings like sadness, anger, joy, and fear with subtle facial expressions?

- Do you experience intense emotions that capture both the attention of others and your attention?

- Do you ignore your emotions or do they play a role in your decision-making process?

If you do not experience any of these, then you may have tamped down or turned off your emotions. If you want to become emotionally intelligent and healthy, then you have to reconnect to those core emotions and accept them, even become comfortable with them.

When developing emotional awareness, you first have to learn how to deal with stress. If you haven't learned how to manage that, then you won't be able to control any of your emotions or even acknowledge them.

Nonverbal Communication

Not only do we need excellent communication skills verbally, but we also need nonverbal communication skills in order to manage our stress and recognize the stress of others. Remember that what you're saying is usually less important than how you're saying it, and the other nonverbal gestures you make, how you're sitting, how fast or loud you're talking, how close you're standing, or the amount of eye contact you're making with the other person all tell them how you're feeling, as well as how they're feeling.

If you want to hold the attention and build a connection with others, then you have to be aware of your nonverbal communication or body language. You have to be able to easily read and respond to their nonverbal cues, too.

Even when we're silent, we have the capability of still sending communication to another person. Think about what you're transmitting, as well as what you're feeling from that person. If you clench your teeth and tell someone you're okay or fine, they're going to know that you're not find or okay. Our nonverbal messages can transmit trust, interest, desire, and excitement or confusion, distrust, fear, and disinterest.

So how can you improve your nonverbal communication?

Well, when you're communicating nonverbally in a successful manner, you're able to manage your stress and recognize the emotions you're feeling, as well as understand the signals you send and receive to and from others. When you're communicating with someone else:

- Focus on that person. If you're not completely focused on that person and instead thinking about what you're going to say or if you're daydreaming, then you will miss many nonverbal cues in your conversation.

- Make eye contact. This communicates interest, and helps maintain the flow of a conversation. It also helps you gauge the other person's response.

- Pay attention to nonverbal cues. Are you sending mixed facial expressions or perhaps using a tone of voice that's completely different than what you want the other person to gather from the situation? Pay attention to your posture and your touch, as well as your gestures. What is the timing and the pace of the conversation? All of these are very important.

Use Humor

Laughter and humor are all natural antidotes to life's daily stress because they lighten up our burdens and help use keep things in perspective. A natural, hearty laugh can reduce your stress levels, elevate your mood, and bring your nervous system into balance.

When you playfully communicate, you:

- Take hardships in stride. You are able to view your frustrations and disappointments from a new perspective and you can survive some everyday annoyances. Laughter also helps you survive the hard times and the setbacks. That's why you see people who are trying to make others laugh after a funeral or after a particularly bad argument. They're attempting to 'lighten the mood'.

- Smooth over differences. We're all different and that means we all have different opinions. Rather than let these opinions and differences upset us, we should use laughter to help us say things that might be difficult to express without causing a fight.

- Simultaneously relax and energize. Communicating in a playful manner helps us relieve fatigue and relax our bodies, allowing us to recharge and accomplish more.

- Become more creative. Laughter helps us loosen up and free ourselves from rigid ways of thinking and being. This allows us to become more creative and see things in a new way.

- So how do you develop playful communication?

- Set aside some regular, quality playtime such as joking, playing or laughing. The more you do it, the easier it becomes.

- Find activities that are enjoyable that loosen you up and help you to embrace that playful side of yourself.

- Practice with babies, animals, young children, and outgoing people who enjoy playful banter themselves.

Resolve Conflict in a Positive Manner

Disagreements and arguments happen in every relationship because two people never have the same opinions, needs, and expectations at the same time. That doesn't have to be a bad thing, though. Resolving your conflicts in a healthy way strengthens the trust between two people because when it's not perceived as a threatening or punishing event, it grows creativity, freedom, and safety.

Managing conflict in a positive, trust-building way is supported by the previous four skills. When you know how to manage stress, become emotionally present and aware, communicate in a nonverbal manner, and use humor and play to distress a situation, you're more equipped to handle an emotionally charged event and defuse many issues before they even escalate.

Here are a few ways you can start resolving conflicts in a trust-building way:

- Stay focused on the present. When you're letting go of old hurts and resentments, you're able to recognize the reality of a current situation and view it in a different light. You view it as a new opportunity to resolve old feelings about conflicts.

- Choose your arguments. Arguments waste a lot of time and energy, especially if they're not resolved in a positive way. Consider what you really believe is worth arguing about and what isn't.

- Forgive. It's a lot easier said than done, I know, but forgiveness is not only for the one who hurt you, but for you. Stop looking to punish or seek revenge on those who hurt you because it's only going to take away from your life.

- End the conflicts that aren't able to be resolved. It takes two in order to be in love, and it takes two for an argument to continue. You are able to step away from an argument and disengage yourself, even if you do not agree with the other person. Sometimes it's just not something that can be resolved right away.

Observation

You should observe how you're reacting to people. Do you rush to judging them before you know all the facts? Are you someone who sees stereotypes? Be honest about how you think and react to others, and try putting yourself in their place. Be more open about their perspectives and their needs.

Work Environment

Do you always seek out attention for accomplishments? Humility is an excellent quality of those who have emotional intelligence. They don't need reassurance from others that they are doing the right thing. It doesn't mean that you lack self-confidence or are shy if you don't want too much recognition. It just means that you realize you're not the most important person on this planet. It's best to give others a chance to shine and focus on them, and stop worrying so much about obtaining praise yourself.

Self-Evaluation

Know your weaknesses and accept that you're not a perfect person, and that you are able to work on some of those areas in your life in order to be a better person. Be honest about this with yourself because it can really change your life.

Examine your Reactions

How do you react in a stressful situation? Are you upset and angry every time something doesn't go your way? Do you blame others are show anger toward them when it's not their fault? Your ability to stay calm and in control during a difficult situation is valued in both the business world and outside of it. Keep your emotions under control and learn how to reduce stress in the moment.

Take Responsibility

When you take responsibility for your actions and apologize to someone directly when you've hurt their feelings or done something wrong, they are more likely to move on and make things right. Be honest with them and sincere about your apology, or it will come across as flat and unwelcoming.

Examine Your Effect on Others

Before you even take an action, examine in your mind how that action will affect those around you. If your decision is going to impact someone else, put yourself in their place. How are they going to feel about this action? Would you want to experience what they're going to experience? If you have to take the action, how can you help them deal with the effects?

Supportive Relationships

It doesn't matter how much time and effort you put into improving your emotional and mental health, you still need others company in order to feel your best. Humans are social and have an emotional need for relationships and a positive connection with someone else. We are not meant to thrive in isolation. We have a social brain that craves companionship, even if the experience for us is shy and distrustful.

When you socially interact with others, you can reduce your stress levels. The key is to find a relationship with someone who is a good listener and supportive of you. You need someone who you can talk to on a regular basis, face-to-face, who will listen to you without having an agenda or telling you how you ought to think or feel. A good listener listens to the emotions behind the words and doesn't interrupt or criticize the other person. The best way to find a good listener is to be one yourself.

Here are a few tips you can use in order to connect with others:

- Get away from the television or the computer screen. These instruments have their place in our lives, but they do not have the same effect as a real expression of interest or a reassuring touch. Communication is a nonverbal experience that requires being in direct contact with others, so never neglect real world interactions.

- Spend time with people you like on a daily basis, face-to-face. Spending time with others that you enjoy helps you relax and get rid of stress. Make time for friends, colleagues, neighbors, and family members that are positive, upbeat and interested in what you're doing. Take time to inquire about the people you meet on a daily basis.

- Volunteer. Not only does volunteering have a positive effect on how you feel about yourself, it has a beneficial effect on the others around you. The meaning and purpose you will find in helping out others will help you feel enriched and expand your horizons. There are no limits when it comes to volunteering. You can volunteer at schools, nonprofits, charitable organizations, churches, and animal shelters.

- Be a joiner. Join in on social action, networking, conversation, and interest groups that meet on a regular basis. This offers wonderful opportunities for you to find others with common interests who could be potential friends.

Chapter 7:
Emotional Intelligence and Personal Relationships

In order to have the best kind of relationships in your life, you need emotional intelligence. In the past chapters you learned what emotional intelligence is and in general how it can be applied. In this chapter, you will learn specifically how you can apply it to benefit the relationships that you have in your personal life.

I am going to start broadly and talk about extended family. First, you will learn how to use emotional intelligence to take control of relationships with people you may not see as often. So, have you been having trouble with your relationship with, for example, your grandmother or mother? Or are you having trouble relating to your brother-in-law or brother who lives across the country – or maybe even across the world? How can you start to mend these relationships so that you can finally have the kind of interaction with these people that you have dreamed of for so long?

Well, the answer is quite simple. It is emotional intelligence: with emotional intelligence you can take control of these family relationships, so that everyone will be happier. There is no need to continue living full of stress, worry, and feelings of sadness because these relationships just did not work out. If you want to get closer to these people in your life, now you can!

First, figure out what relationships in your life you would like to work on. Think about which relationships are leaving you feeling unhappy because they have not worked out. Figure out which relationships could help you to be a happier person if they were different. Then, act on your wish to mend these relationships. You can just start with one relationship if you do not want to take on too much at one time.

Next, start reaching out to the person that you want to build your relationship with. If you are already planning to see them, don't stress out or worry – even if this is what you normally do. When you see them, or when you talk to them over the phone, try to gauge their emotions. Try to be aware of what they are feeling, and how they are reacting to what you are saying to them – even to just seeing you in general. Your words, actions, and reactions should all depend on how you see them behaving. The way they behave is a great way to tell what they are feeling inside. If you are experienced at reading people's emotions, you will be able to easily figure out how they are feeling and then use this knowledge to both of your benefits. They will benefit from your emotional intelligence as well. Since you are using emotional intelligence, you will be less likely to have a misunderstanding, or say something to them that they will interpret in the wrong way. And, even better, you will be more likely to meet and talk again soon. With emotional intelligence, you are well on your way to building a stronger, healthier relationship with this family member – even if you feel like you don't know them that well because you don't see them every day (or even every year).

The truth is that extended family relationships can be hard to maintain for these very reasons – you just don't know them as well as your other family members. For this reason, it is especially important that all your attention and focus in on them during those few hours each month, or maybe each year, that you get to spend with them. In our busy lives, it is far too often that our attention is elsewhere – making it possible to use emotional intelligence in these situations.

You need to fully focus on the person you are talking to and spending time with, so that you can make up for lost time. Maybe there is something that has happened in their lives since you have last seen them that you don't even know about. Well, the truth is that maybe you are never going to find out about it. Or, at least you are not going to find about all of the details that the people closer to this person know. However, that doesn't mean that you can't read and figure out generalizations about what has gone on from their face, their voice, and their actions – and sometimes, to be honest, that is all you need to know. With this knowledge, you can better understand their actions. It will help you not to lash out at them if you understand the motives for their behavior or harsh words. And it will help you to treat them the way you yourself would want to be treated if you were in their situation – to say the things that will help them through whatever it is that they are going through.

Next, let's think about the relationships with the people you see every day. These relationships encounter plenty of problems of their own. You can build back up a broken relationship by trying to understand what the other person is feeling, and by using this knowledge to interact with them accordingly. For example, take someone who is always fighting with their spouse. In this case, it may be that the two people are not reading each other's emotions correctly. In order to mend the situation, a good first step would be for them to pay attention to the other person's emotions.

In all family relationships, you may have to assess the situation and see if you are focusing on yourself too much. Perhaps you are just wrapped up in worry about your own problems. Or maybe you are worried about what other people think about you. The truth is that in order to have better relationships with these people, you will have to stop focusing on yourself and start focusing on them. You can focus on yourself and them – the interactions you are having together. This will make it harder to misread their face or voice, which is exactly what you want. You want to be able to read them correctly so you know how to act around them and how to talk with them.

Taking control of the personal relationships in your life is all about helping relationships to work so that you can be happy again. It is all about taking your thoughts about what you want the relationships in your life to be like – and making these hopes and dreams become a reality. With a higher emotional intelligence, you can do this easily. In fact, you probably won't believe how easy it is with emotional intelligence.

Right now, you might be thinking that there are other relationships in your life as well – so what about those? These relationships are very different from the relationships that you have with your family. Probably the other largest category of relationships, the one that most people can relate to, are the relationships you have with the people you work with. These professional relationships can be difficult as well – especially if you are in a tough work situation, or a job that you don't really like. But no matter what, knowing how to take control of these professional relationships is very important. In the next chapter, you will learn how emotional intelligence can help you with this.

Chapter 8:
Emotional Intelligence and Professional Relationships

Now you are going to learn how a higher emotional intelligence can help your relationships with your boss and your coworkers. First, let's talk about your boss or supervisor at work. This relationship is obviously very important – and one that you don't want to mess up. Sometimes, this relationship can be very hard – you are trying to act the right way, but one little mistake can send you worrying that your job might be on the line.

So, to prevent this excess worrying, you will need to acquire some emotional intelligence. If you can tell what your boss is thinking and feeling, then even if they aren't saying it you will have a better idea of what is happening. This will prevent you from thinking you are getting fired when in reality they are just having a bad day. It is important to understand people's emotions because these emotions will show in their faces – and you don't want to jump to the wrong conclusion that these emotions are because of you.

Emotional intelligence is all about focusing on what is going on around you – in specific the other people around you and anything about them that could tell you how they are feeling. This is very important in the work situation – there are a lot of people and your ability to interact with them may mean the difference between keeping the job you love and losing it. So how can having more emotional intelligence help you to successfully interact with your coworkers in a way that is both productive and right for the specific job situation you are in? Well, there are so many ways which emotional intelligence can help you interact with coworkers. If you are working as a group with other employees, it is time to make sure you are using your emotional intelligence to the best of your abilities – because you are definitely going to need it.

Prior to this we have basically been talking about relationships where only two people are involved. Now, in the workplace, we are talking about social situations where you are required to work with multiple people – whether this means several people or a whole group. So, what does this mean in terms of using emotional intelligence? Well, unfortunately this means that it is going to be much harder. The reason you will likely find it more difficult is that you simply have more people around you, which means you have more emotions and feelings to try to gauge to the best of your ability.

This just means that it is even more important than before to practice mindfulness and to learn to come to the workplace completely stress-free. If you are not stressed, it will be so much easier to use your emotional intelligence when you are in a group of people. You also need to completely focus on what is going on around you in order to practice emotional intelligence around more than one person. If you have developed these skills which were outlined earlier in the book, it will make it so much easier to work with others. Working with others requires that you understand their emotions because if you can't you either won't know how to interact with them, or, more likely, you will interact with them in the wrong way.

If someone is having a bad day, or something has just happened in your life, then you will need to adjust the way you talk to them accordingly. The failure to do this can result in difficulty working as a group, arguments, or even a fight. However, if you can do this, then the group will work so much more smoothly. Everything will go smoothly because you all are taking the time to understand each other, and to tailor interactions to each specific person depending on the way that person is interacting with you. It is important to be able to look at a person and decide quickly how you should interact with them to achieve the results you want – which in this case is harmony throughout the group which will allow you all to work together and get the job done.

If you are a supervisor at work, whether you are just supervising a small group for a simple project or a larger number of people for a long time, then emotional intelligence is especially important. Without emotional intelligence, how will you ensure that everything with the group is running smoothly? You will get so much work done if you have higher emotional intelligence. Remember, if you don't feel like you currently have a high emotional intelligence, there is no need to fret. Earlier in this book tips were given for how to successfully develop your emotional intelligence. So no matter how lacking you feel that you are in this area, these tips will be just the help that you need. Follow them to have more emotional intelligence in no time – and all the relationships in your life will benefit from it.

In this chapter you learned some tips for using emotional intelligence to help you navigate the difficulties of the workplace. In the last chapter, you learned about using emotional intelligence when at home for the benefit of the relationships that you have there. Now, in the last chapter of the book, we will be talking about emotional intelligence and social skills in general. You will learn how to use your emotional intelligence to have better social skills. So, do you feel that your social skills could use improvement? Well, if you do, then this will be an important section for you. Emotional intelligence will help you to interact with all types of people better.

Chapter 9:
Emotional Intelligence and Social Skills

In the last chapters you have been learning about how to interact with people you know – whether that means close family members or at least people you know of and have seen before. However, that seems to give the impression that emotional intelligence can only be beneficial to relationships you have with people that you already know – however well you may know them. The truth is that emotional intelligence can actually help with any social interaction – even if you don't have an actual relationship with the person and never will. What do I mean by this? Well, let's give some quick examples from everyday life that most people can probably relate to.

If you are, for example, at the store and interacting with a stranger, then emotional intelligence can help. If you are going to see a doctor, emotional intelligence can help. Emotional intelligence can help with all social interactions that you have with anyone, anywhere. If you have emotional intelligence, you can use it to develop your social skills.

So, in what way are you looking to develop your social skills? Are you hoping to have an easier time deciding how to interact with a specific person or type of person? Do you want new social situations to be smoother for you – you want to minimize worrying about them even though they are something you have never experienced before? Or do you want to know what to say in difficult social situations when it seems there are just no words? Well, emotional intelligence can help you in all of these situations.

With emotional intelligence, you will know what to say and how to behave – no matter how foreign the situation is. You will know how to interact with different types of people – and how to decide to interact with someone that you are about to meet. You will also know how to stop worrying about new situations and experiences. How can emotional intelligence help with all of this? Well, it really is simple. As you have already learned, emotional intelligence helps you to tell what other people's emotions are. And in all of these situations, what you really need is to be able to know what the other person is feeling. If you know this, then the interaction will come so much more naturally. Emotional intelligence truly is a wonderful skill to have in these situations!

So, let's start with the first situation and elaborate just a little so that you can get a better idea of this. Is there a specific person that you are having trouble knowing how to interact with? If this is the case, then you can stop worrying about it. Simply use your emotional intelligence when you are in a situation with this person. Try to read their emotions, and interact accordingly. With emotional intelligence, even if you have never met this person before the interaction will still be smooth. Even if you don't get along with this specific type of person, with emotional intelligence, you will be able to make things go better than they normally would. Try to understand them, and think about where they are coming from. Forget everything else you are thinking about, and focus your attention on them, and how you think it would be best to interact with them. This will be sure to help turn an uncomfortable situation into a much more comfortable one.

Next, are you worrying about a social situation because it is new and different? Emotional intelligence will help you to get through even the newest of situations. It is all about being able to learn about the people you are with, even if you have never met them. How do you use emotional intelligence to learn about them? Well, you need to try to read their emotions.

Emotions can be deducted based on how they are speaking, how they look (happy, sad, uncomfortable, nervous) and so much more. If you look closely enough, you can learn about someone you have never met. It is definitely possible – you just have to be focused and you have to be living in the present moment.

Now, let's talk a little about the last scenario that was posed as a question above. This scenario involves difficult social situations when it seems there are no words to say. In a situation like this, it will be extremely important to try to figure out the other person's emotions. Then, you will know what to say based on how they seem to be feeling. All in all, emotional intelligence can really help you with social interaction in so many ways. These were only three examples – there are so many more ways that it can help you. So, this is just another reason to learn how to develop your emotional intelligence.

Conclusion

Being aware of your emotional intelligence levels allows you to branch out further and start educating yourself and practicing with the different techniques that were provided to you in this eBook. Remember that emotional intelligence has nothing to do with your IQ, but it does have everything to do with how people will perceive you and how you will feel about yourself.

Those who have a high emotional intelligence are able to be successful in their personal and business relationships because they are able to understand their spouses, children, and coworkers on a much better level. Just with a few facial expressions, we can convey whether we're sad or happy or if we're just feeling bored. When you're able to read someone's emotions, you'll be able to gauge their reaction to what you're about to say much easier. This could save you a lot of grief and hassle in the future.

So now that you have learned all about emotional intelligence and social skills, emotional intelligence and relationships, how to apply emotional intelligence, and of course, most importantly, how to develop it, the next step is to start putting it into practice in your everyday life. Emotional intelligence can help you greatly in so many situations. No matter how hard a situation may seem, with emotional intelligence it will be easier to get through. Take what you have learned from this book and use it to start living a better life today. It is not hard, and it will definitely be very rewarding!

Made in the USA
Monee, IL
10 March 2020

22987059R00115